THE PERFECT LOVE OF THE FATHER

for the less perfect me

LOIS

The Perfect Love of the Father for the less perfect me

Copyright © 2021 Lois

First edition 2021

ISBN 978-0-620-92312-5

ISBN 978-0-620-92314-9 (e-book)

All rights reserved

No part of this work may be reproduced or transmitted in any form or by any means, electronic, photographic or mechanical, including photocopying and recording on record, tape or laser disk, on microfilm, via the Internet, by e-mail, or by any other information storage or retrieval system, without prior written permission from the copyright owner.

The author has made every effort to obtain permission for and acknowledge the use of copyrighted material. Refer all enquiries to the author.

Set in Minion Pro 11/13

Printed and bound in South Africa by Print on Demand (Pty) Ltd 5

Koets str, Parow Industria, 7493

GEDIG

Sr Lois...
'n Ware vriendin en getroue metgesel,
dit kan iedereen wat haar pad kruis jou vertel.
Vol inspanning smeek sy om genade oor my verkeerde weë.
In haar liggaam en haar gees ervaar sy ander se lyding en hartseer
Deur dik en dun stap sy saam in nood,
met hand in sak voorsien sy ruim;
sit op tafel brood.
Soos 'n rigter van vervloë tyd,
bid sy verborge sondes uit.
Sy ag haar lewe so gering,
met lof sal sy 'n ander hulde bring;
soos 'n engel vir pasiënte in hospital.
Haar woorde genees die kwaad in elke saal.
Soos'n oase in die woestyn
vloei lewende water uit haar fontein.
Soek die Here dan 'n rein kanaal,
 gebruik Hy haar om ander uit
moedverloor se vlak te haal.
Mag die Here haar seën in al haar harde werk.
Sy is altyd daar om ander te versterk.
Haar hartsverlange en gebed is
dat die Heer almal se siele red.
Geliefde suster van die Here.
Die suster Lois...
Deborah Will;
mede stryder

1. BACKGROUND

It's a beautiful evening outside. The sun has taken up its resting place and stars are shining brightly across the vast dark sky. Pity though, that the lights of the cityscape are dimming the brightness of the stars.

My back is pressed tightly against the hard-outside wall of the bedroom. I am mesmerised by the cool swimming pool water. Once again, lift my gaze to the sky... My inner being yearns for the time when I could still pray and have wonderful conversations with the FATHER OF THE UNIVERSE and bask in His tangible presence.If only, I could pray like that!

The inner turmoil is raging so hard within myself, that I am leaning on the wall for help to stand up straight. The water should bring me a kind of soothing, but there seems to be no solace in anything on this night.

A song was composed, Psalm 37 verse 1 "By the rivers of Babylon where we sat down. Yeah, we wept, when we remembered Zion... How shall we sing the Lord's song in a strange land" Tonight, I miss Jesus with everything inside of me!Tonight, I find myself in a strange land...

There are no more chances left for me, I have lost the Lord as well as His Sweet Holy Spirit... The only thing still helping me are the prayers of my mother and father. Every so often I share my hurt with them and then I do experience some kind of comfort. They also are only seeing the tip of this iceberg; how did I get here... where did I take the wrong turn?

Like in a picture book it plays out in my mind's eye. I was 21 years old when I accepted Jesus as my personal Saviour, and everything changed in my life. My parents had been praying for years for my salvation in Jesus... According to Scripture you should actually be 'born again'.

John 3 verse 3:"Jesus replied,"Very truly I tell you,no one can see the Kingdom of God unless they are born again."

That is what I experienced, and I grew in His stature. There were many things that I had to give up, but I gained so much more. I still vividly see myself and mother Babs, my spiritual mother at that point in time, walking side by side. It was only a week before she moved to her forever home with Jesus. We are walking along her small path, amongst the roses. Suddenly, her eyes fixing on mine she says: "my child, beware of the wide road". I felt annoyed, there is but only Jesus Christ the Lord on my path, whatever does she mean? Years later, the Scripture became clear.

Mathew 11 verse 6; "Blessed are those who are not OFFENDED by My Word" Jesus himself said that.

Now, here I am, married to an unsaved man. Without Jesus, without hope; had I but taken heed and prayed;

Matthew 6 verse 13 "lead us not into temptation,but deliver us from the evil one".

But pride, the biggest enemy of the cross, had tempted me to a deep level of despair! I, the wonderful true believer who on many occasions, would look down on others who were weak. Yes! Many times, I had been irritated with many around me who were 'slow' and yet, tonight, they are still serving our Master, whilst I am lost, pressed against a dead wall crying for help.

The atmosphere inside the house is laden thick with anger, unhappiness, and dissatisfaction, I could not breathe in there. Outside, here, is some relief.

The biggest problem: "How could dad get married barely two years after our mother died? And that, to a woman who could never do or be what our mother was?" Hours spent talking about their mother. Articles published in the newspaper. And he indulged them, to stay within their favour. Published in large print – their wedding anniversary. How much he still loves her, his departed wife, already three years gone. Also, read at my workplace, in the tearoom. Some laugh, some take pity on me, some would openly remark: "rather you than me, I never want to be caught in a marriage like that".

Yes, tonight, I heard, a phone call from the Karoo, which is now counting against me. I was there for Christmas and as always, father trusted the Lord to give the Word, because that is the only time, he still has to get Word from Jesus through to us. In all sincerity he brought the message: "which star are you following tonight... the one to Bethlehem,where Jesus was born, or the shooting star across the Karoo skies... You can see that it is burning out... it is falling... it's light is fading." At that precise moment the phone rang, it was, my husband to be. At that point I was still with Jesus or should I say, I still heard His Sweet Voice from time to time.

At the very moment the phone rang, I knew that this issue would be a shooting star issue.

When the time for, asking permission to marry, came, my mother begged: "Darling, you've never been married and especially you, who've had such a free lifestyle, are you really up for taking on a husband with two children (the son, at the time, was 21 and the daughter about 11)? "Yes mom, I am ready for this challenge".

Daddy said nothing, he had spoken some time before... "Darling, what do you make of it that the Scripture warns against it, that a believer cannot pull the same wagon as a non-believer?"

2 Corinthians 6 verse 14; "Do not be bound together with unbelievers; for what partnership have righteousness and lawlessness, or what fellowship has light with darkness?

Verse 15 Or what harmony has Christ with Belial, or what has a believer in common with an unbeliever?

"Daddy, it's quite possible for him to give his life to the Lord." Dad again replied calmly, but quite assertive "The Scripture also states, 'who's to say, he would turn his life to the Lord?"

1 Corinthians 7 verse 16;" For how do you know, O wife, whether you will save your husband? Or how do you know, O husband, whether you will save your wife?

Our conversation ended right there. Dad gave it over in the hands of The Almighty... If you don't listen, go on and feel... and don't I feel it tonight, right here, my stubbornness is hurting me! Tonight, when I look up to the stars, I can see, in the spaces between them, how mommy was trusting right up to the end... The wedding dress was hastily bought from Foschini and that very evening she still proclaimed, "The Lord can still put an end to this marriage".

On my wedding day I could see how difficult it was for my father to give me away as a bride. Mom's arms were hanging heavily from her shoulders, as if she was truly deeply weighted down with worry.

Only the Master knows the depth of the hurt, when watching your beloved daughter, make the biggest mistake of her life. To my parents, the wedding was more like a funeral. Even for me, it wasn't a truly wonderful day. I know, I am making a mistake. I longed to get out of it, but it was as if ropes, were binding us together.

Today I discovered, it truly was ropes that bound me!

Out of desperation I spoke to my mother in law, told her how terrible it was to be in a house with a husband and children constantly making you feel, not welcome. I am not allowed to hang any of my own paintings or things I hold dear, lest there be huge disconsolation. Everything, must remain as it was, even the meals, food habits.

Fortunately for them, there was a full time cleaner, who'd been "taught according to their hands". Even she would only speak to me when necessary.

When I open the door, it would be as if everything changed. A silence fell onto the house. My husband not home, very often, as he led his life: sports, sports and then still the party after the sports. That, I have never known... my father would never return home at 2am or 3am, twice three times a week.

Mother in law answered me rather self-assuredly "child, I am a really good fortune teller" and she subsequently told me she had gone to a Muslim fortune teller, also, before our wedding, who said something to the effect of "you will have a fairy tale marriage" and also that "the illness your mother has, won't be terminal".

Lost for words, I walked away from the telephone. So, this is why I could not be free.

I knew no-one, who was trained in the field of these dark forces or how to fight them with in the Power of Jesus. I now knew how Samson must have felt when all his might was taken away.

Judges 16 verse 20; "Then she called, Samson the Philistines are upon you! He awoke from his sleep and thought. I'll go out as before and shake myself free. But HE DID NOT KNOW THAT THE LORD HAD LEFT HIM."

Today, I had the shock of my life. I knew, fortune telling has binding powers, over your life. It must be cut off my life, in the Power of the

Name of Jesus. But tonight, I cannot pray. I realise the reason why I couldn't get out of the marriage. Since the night we asked my parents, permission for marriage. My dad, had twice, been rushed with an ambulance to the City. His health turned, very bad, suddenly. Because I was unfaithful to the Lord, these dark powers were free to cause havoc with their dirty deeds.

As in Spiritual language, "the devil claimed me, and I allowed it". Samson's eyes were out... Two days after the wedding, it was as if the star had burnt out. My husband didn't want me close to him. We went on honeymoon much later, which was very uncomfortable. My heart felt torn into a thousand pieces. My first marriage, at 35, something I have always dreamed about. He only wants to go fishing or go home... speaks to me only when necessary. The star has shot, because the devil that made him fall in love with me, only to destroy me, had finished his job.

As in John 10 verse 10 "The thief comes only to steal and kill and destroy;"

Reader please bear with me; I have to write the truth, to warn those who read about this, how serious it is to take the Master's warnings into contempt. It is a bitter price to pay and who knows if you will be able to bear it?

My mood is very heavy tonight; almost too heavy to carry. His voice sounds through the window; "come in, you have been sitting outside for long enough." I feel the weight of ten mountains. I dragged myself, to go inside, with no hope in my heart.

The next morning, mother calls. "Darling, what is going on, don't you want to open up and speak to us? Dad and I have been praying for you all through the night; we can feel your turmoil." The prayers of parents cannot be measured in any currency. It is worth far more than gold! "Oh mom, things are not as I want."

2. BACK TO THE FATHER'S HEART

I feel the need growing inside of me to get inside of a church. That Sunday I randomly joined a small Baptist Church in the area. What an experience it was! I believe it was my date with the love of the Father of the Universe. There was a visiting preacher from America, and he brought this message.

Nehemiah 9; Verse 17 They refused to listen and failed to remember the miracles you performed among them. They became stiff-necked and, in their rebellion, appointed a leader in order to return to their slavery. But you are a forgiving God, gracious and compassionate, slow to anger and abounding in love. Therefore you did not desert them,

Verse 18 even when they cast for themselves an image of a calf and said, 'This is your god, who brought you up out of Egypt,' or when they committed awful blasphemies.

Verse 19 Because of Your great compassion you did not abandon them in the wilderness. By day, the pillar of cloud did not fail to guide them on their path, nor the pillar of fire by night to shine on the way they were to take."

The message had been about Moses.

The preacher went on:

Exodus 32 verse 19; ...and Moses anger burned, and he threw the tablets from his hands and shattered them at the foot of the mountain.

Verse 20 And he took the calf which they had made and burned it with fire, and ground it to powder, and scattered it over the surface of the water, and made the sons of Israel drink it."

The preacher went on to explain the Word further...

Moses threw the tablets with the ten commandments down; he burnt the golden calf, destroy it totally. Some-times you made your own plans and worship it. (like I did, with this marriage)

Exodus 32 verse 31: Then Moses returned to the Lord, and said," Alias , this people has commited a great sin,and they have made a god of gold for themselves.

Verse32 "But now, if Thou wilt forgive their sins-and if not, please blot me out from Thy book which Thou hast written!"

Then I saw, in my mind's eye how my own father went to the Lord to plead for the preservation of my soul... And the Lord once again gave Moses the ten commandments.

The preacher said;" there are people here today in this service, who think they will not be granted another chance, who had, against the will of the Father, married a non-believer, yet the Father gave the Israelites another chance..." The preacher then invited us: "give your life to the Lord again today... THERE IS GRACE FOR YOU ONCE AGAIN FROM THE FATHER".

What a sweet moment? With my whole heart I took that Word for myself and invited Jesus back into my life. After that, we had the Holy Communion. Happiness entered my being like a stream, and I felt once again the love, forgiveness and acceptance of my Heavenly Father. As I walked out of there, I was in the clouds. I felt as light as a feather...

I squeezed the hand of the preacher and told him, the message was directly for me, I thanked him. If only that preacher could truly know what his message has brought into my life!!! Total turn around, from falling apart, from the ashes to His Kingdom; from hopeless to fearless and filled with power; from being satan's bait to warrior in Jesus Christ; from crying, to glowing with His love...

I walked into the house still high on those clouds... nothing mattered except for the Love of Jesus Christ the Lord, which was covering me completely.

On Monday morning I gave my parents a call. "Mom, I gave my life to Jesus once again and it is truly, just like the first time, I feel so happy and content."

All of my bibles and Christian literature had been out away in the attic of the farmhouse. Still covered in dust my parents brought it back to me. Glory to the Lord! As I cleaned the dust off them, I read, and I hugged the Word against my bosom. Now it is my most treasured gift. Oh, dearest Lord, how could I have traded you for the things of the world?

1 Samuel 8 verse 18;" Then you will cry out in that day because of your king whom you have have chosen for yourself, but the Lord will not answer you in that day."

Verse 19 NEVERTHELESS, THE PEOPLE REFUSED TO LISTEN TO THE VOICE OF SAMUEL, AND THEY SAID," NO BUT THERE SHALL BE A KING OVER US,

Verse 20 THAT WE ALSO MAY BE LIKE ALL THE NATIONS

Samuel heard from the Lord how they would suffer under such a king, but they insisted on having a king like the people... I wanted to be married because everyone around is married... and all the while I had been given Biblical advice:

Isiah 54:5 "For your Maker is your husband –
the Lord Almighty is His name –
the Holy One of Israel is your Redeemer; He is called the God of all the earth."

When I obeyed, the Holy Word. My eyes on the Master and Father of the Universe, heavenly happiness was upon me and a deep sense of contentment, which is not of this world. If you should be single, you can live a very happy life, I can confess to that. The Father can bestow upon you such fulfilment that you would not even have a yearning for children of your own.

My brother's and my two sisters' children are just like my own. They bring me so much joy. They allowed me to be a part of their lives.
Then there are my spiritual children who crawled deep into my heart.

Isaiah 54 verse 1"Sing, barren woman,
you who never bore a child; burst into song, shout for joy, you who were never in labour;
because more are the children of the desolate woman than of her who has a husband,
says the Lord.
Verse 2: "Enlarge the place of your tent, stretch your tent curtains wide, do not hold back;"

Yes, if someone should read this and think "the Father neglected me, with, not giving me children or a marriage, it is not true. Today, I am nearly sixty, not having, children of my own, but I have so many children; spiritual children as well as those of my own family. Many hours spend in prayer for them. It is then when the Master reveals, how to pray and fight in secret. and in so doing to change the course of their history, on my knees.

Oh, that first Sunday, after I gained my New Life in Christ back, I walked out of the house with pride, Bible in my hand. It was as though my life had begun anew; words cannot describe it. The Master gave me another chance! His Blood had forgiven my stubborn sins, my wilfulness; He wiped my disobedience away with His blood.

Oh, how sweet is the relief when the weight of your sins is gone. The, pressure of what you have done unto your parents by going against the Lord's will, is forgiven Friends had pleaded with me, but the "me" just steamed forward… That "me " is now lying broken, on the ground, still, the Lord reaches out to me with His Mighty arms to pick up this naughty child to blow His new Life into her lungs. Strength to carry on… Life in abundance… Heavenly life flowing through your veins; once again your prayers start to flow, and He hears, and He answers you. The enemy… that old devil… cannot walk all over you and hurt you,anymore.

Now, there is a High Priest, Christ Jesus, who intervenes for me and teaches me all the ways to resist the enemy. What a wonderful Father, who created the earth in seven days. He now is my Shepherd, and he carries me in His arms through all the dangers exist.

Slowly, I begin the journey; I have to be very careful, for I am still on the enemy's terrain.

I am writing my experiences, in very basic terms. I, had to learn from scratch. It, is not a studied, subject, but learning on the way. The, Holy Spirit the best Teacher, using people or teaching me, personally.

3. SECOND CHANCE IS NOW A REALITY...

The first thoughts that came to me in a soft and tender voice, I heard very clearly and with great peace and joy were the words "hyssop branch". I realised this, the voice of the Holy Spirit. Very excitedly I began researching the Bible for the meaning.
Exodus 12 verse 22 "Take a bunch of hyssops, dip it into the blood in the basin and put some of the blood on the top and on both sides of the door frames
Verse 23 When the Lord goes through the land to strike down the Egyptians,he will see the blood on the top and sides of the doorframe and will pass over that doorway, and he will not permit the destroyer to enter your houses and strike you down."

Master, whatever could this mean? Please give me guidance; through Your Spirit please make it clear to me what it is that I must learn! I prayed very sincerely.

And sure, as only our Master can blow the very breath of the Almighty His Holy Spirit, I began to understand. Through my husband and his children, who were so busy with the things of the dark underworld, the darkness and curses of Egypt, as the Word calls it, crept into our home through the doorposts of our home. Father, what should I do now?

The next Saturday evening I was alone, my husband and his children, gone out to a rugby game at Newlands. While on my way home, the thought entered my mind, that I should dip my hands in oil and touch all the doors and windows and that I should pray: "Lord, seal this with Your Blood". There was doubt in me,but something was urging me,on. Later on,I studied the bible, concerning the oil. I heard, from other people of the faith, how very powerful this action is!

Exodus 40 verse 9: "Take the anointing oil and anoint the tabernacle and everything in it; consecrate it and all its furnishings, and it will be holy."

The daughter came home, early evening. I immediately knew something was wrong. Later on, I phoned my sister-in-law, if they might know what had happened to him, as he still wasn't home. The daughter was resting her head in my lap, she was so embarrassed, and then I knew, the father was visiting his previous girlfriend and her family; he had all but forgotten he is a married man now. I felt powerless, deeply humiliated but also very angry. Late at night, I heard car doors banging, I was foolish (I gained much more wisdom) and I stormed out, to see that it was her brother and him. "What kind of people are you, who don't have respect for a marriage?!" I blurted out in my humiliation… (MISTAKE!!) Later, I learnt never to be confrontational when they were filled with liquor and returned from such places. A softer approach would gain much better results. They were actually, waiting for my angry response, or put into other words, the devil wanted it. The both of them started cursing "you are crazy" and other words which I couldn't even type here. I had never encountered this kind of behaviour; I have never been yelled at in such a crusty way. All the way inside, my husband was cursing, but once inside, he became calm. The anointing oil and His Blood were now at work; binding that devil inside of him. But all of a sudden, he got hold of me, pushed me against the kitchen door and he put his hands around my neck, starting to choke me in anger. In some way I managed to cut loose and shouted, "I am going to call my father right now to come and fetch me!" At that moment, it was the only place I had wanted to be; in the safety of and protection of their love. While I made the call and my father had already answered, my husband pulled the phone from its socket and threw it on the floor, so that the call was cut off before we could speak.

Later on, everything became clear to me; for some reason, I neglected to anoint the back door of the house, that is how the enemy could manifest there. But in the rest of the house, it was powerless.

Afterwards, I heard from my mother that my father didn't sleep at all that night. He was wondering what went on. He only heard me say "hello" before everything went silent. Mother tried to calm him down by telling him that I had a habit of walking through malls and would call from time to time from a payphone to tell her what I'd seen or eaten and that she thought it might have been the reason .It was a bit late for walking in the mall. We never talked about that night and what had actually happened, again.

What suffering my father must have gone through that night on the farm, wondering about his youngest child. At least he was comforted by the thought I am back with Jesus Christ. Then I learnt the following lesson…

I woke up suddenly, realizing it is past midnight. My husband asleep, next to me. I knew I should rush to the front door. The same urgency from that Saturday, was pushing me to get out of bed and go! I smeared my fingers with oil (at that point I had only ordinary cooking oil at home. It was only in later years that I started using olive oil.), I anointed the door post whilst praying in the name of Jesus Christ. The Power of His Blood to protect us.

Suddenly I became aware of footsteps coming up to the door and a key turning in the keyhole. I ran back to the bedroom to hear the front door opening. It was just seconds, or I would have been caught in the passage, by his son, returning home. My heart was pounding while I slipped, quickly but silently back into bed. I prayed, and talked to the Master. Why now? Why so urgently, Master? What is going on?

A few days passed normally. I go to work, come home, and go directly to our bedroom. The daughter at that time had been 12 years old and she would sometimes make a little conversation with me when she was home. My husband had been working late shifts, or else he might have been at some sports event. She had his consent to visit where and how long she wanted. It always felt as though everyone just wanted to flee.

Tired and worn out, from a hard day at work, I return home. On the way home, I prayed "Oh Lord, please let peace be in our home." The new live-in, cleaner, came from her room, as I opened the door. "Madam! Tonight, I want to talk to you. I can't take it any longer, the way the son is talking about you. He would sometimes ask if the "horrible name" is at home when he refers to you. He would never use nice and proper language when he refers to you, I find Madam so kind and pleasant, I just can't take it anymore that he speaks about you like that."

I thanked her for speaking her mind and assured her that I would do something about it, but I left it at that for the time being. In my mind's eye, I witness the curtain being lifted from the darkness surrounding us. My thoughts go back to the urgency of the other night, when I was summoned to anoint the front door with oil.

It is Friday evening, and everything seems pleasantly peaceful as if His peace is covering us. The fire is burning, and the stars are shining brightly. We are sitting at the outside table under the veranda. On summer evenings I love to take a swim every so often. Both children are out for the weekend and the cleaner also has her weekend off and not at home. But oh my... it was short-lived. All of a sudden, like a shuddering of wind, my husband's temper flared. Just as a chameleon changes colour, so changes his mood, in the blink of an eye. All of a sudden, everything is wrong: the salad, the bread; myself; a lot of things are being shouted at me. I, say a sad prayer: "Master, what happened? I don't understand it; please give me wisdom as to where this evil wind has come from?" I have not even ended my prayer when the phone rang. At that point we were mostly using the landlines in the house. It was the son... just checking in to say he was longing for him, my husband said. (The boy was visiting his fiancé in the neighbouring town.)

I begin to understand. There must be a way to use your thoughts with evil power, to send, out to cause a rift between two people, especially if there is envy in your heart. I think that it might be something to the liking of causing a spell, because the boy had just been here a while ago, it must have come from him! The barbecued meat is cold... no one feels like eating any more. Steeped in silence we go to bed. One thing I am now certain of, that something evil is working through the son aimed at our marriage.

Another week starts in silence... sleep, eat, work, pray. The wonderful aroma of the Friendship of Jesus carries me through and empowers me to tackle the bull by the horns. When I find my husband to be in a good spirit, I mention to him about his son's nasty way of talking about me and to me. I also mention that I feel we cannot live like that under one roof. The two of us approach his bedroom, which is always closed, heavy metal music blasting inside. Nervously my husband pushed open the door. "Son... can we talk?"

Yes, the boy feels he just cannot stand me and that is that. All of us agree that there really isn't anything we can do about it. He did apologise, though. Truly! We ascertain that it had already started on the Sunday before our wedding. His eyes were swollen, and the cleaner told us that he had been at his mother's grave, crying. It was never mentioned to either myself or his father that he despised me.

I had always thought he was just a quiet person. He was 22 and engaged. It had never dawned on me to ask the children how they had felt about us getting married, although I did have an open conversation with the daughter a few weeks ago.

My husband decided it was time for new bedroom cupboards for the children's rooms, because just before our wedding he had had a new barbecue area built as well as new cupboards for the main bedroom. The cupboards were really old, for when their mother was alive, they never had money for such things. The monthly cost of living had swallowed their whole income. Now they had a bit of inheritance money for these things. The daughter's room had been done first and looked beautiful. Passionately she was packing and tidying everything. Then it was the son's turn. The son had been asked to clear his cupboards but instead he left on the Friday straight from work for his fiancé's house.

I had the day free from work and when the workers arrived to do the cupboards, we found his cupboards still full of his things; nothing had been cleared! The daughter then helped me to quickly, clear out, the cupboard. The horrible pornography I found there... I pleaded for the Lord's protection over me to keep me clean. I said to the girl, I do not understand this... your dad also just wants to help you guys! she replied "I understand, my brother, I also felt the same. When mom was alive, none of these things ever happened. It all started since you came." (Just a piece of advice for someone reading here, should you venture into a second marriage with children!)

So, this explains a lot, as well as his animosity towards me? Shivers ran up and down my spine. I was cold right down to my toes. What do I see there...? a CD-cover was lying at my feet. The title "The lie of John 3 verse16". So, it hit me, somewhere he was busy with the occult and the dark underworld.

"OH LORD, HELP ME" was my silent prayer. The daughter saw what I was looking at, she said nonchalantly "Yes, he has many powers. Some of his friends can move out of their bodies. I also have powers... I can make lightbulbs fuse."

So, this was the reason why I had to come and clear the cupboards, it was that I would discover this secret. Yes, Abba Father had known, that is why He had me anoint the doors, day, and night.

As is written in the Word: so that the curses of Egypt cannot harm you, smear the Blood of the Lamb on your doorposts."

With "Oh is that so?" I left the room to get some fresh air. My legs felt lame. I have heard about devil worshippers, but I have never had any experience with that.

I only know this, that John 3 verse 16 is a most beautiful piece of Scripture: "For God so loved the world that he gave his one and only Son, that whoever believes in him shall not perish but have eternal life."

If you should listen to music depicting that verse as a lie, your heart is very far gone from the Truth…

The cleaner asked me what was wrong, and I told her about the words on the C.D. She felt it was meaningless, but I felt the uneasiness stirring in my being! There was huge danger looming, but the brave old me had told my mother that I was up for this marriage… At that time, I had not known about satan,s hidden agenda, to ruin my Christian life in totality…

With my mind still heavily burdened with worry and full of unanswered questions, I walked out of the Christian bookshop. At this point I could not even recall how I ended up at this particular shopping complex to get to the book shop. It was as though something had led me there. I have not eaten anything; something was keeping me away from food. (It would only be later, that I would come to learn the value of fasting and prayer.) The book, I now had with me, had so much as jumped out from the rest, so that I bought it instinctively. I could not wait to start reading it and went into the first coffee shop I encountered. I knew nothing about the author or the book itself, but from my core I felt a hurry to get into it. I look at the title again: 'He came to set the captives free' by Rebecca Brown. I see it addresses the occult and how the Lord had helped her, with His Blood and His Holy Name. I start to read very attentively, and I see a lot of what I had just experienced. One of the hymns we often sing "Only Jesus and you will go on this way". Truly, I have now discovered how He is leading the way to get to the correct aid. I was literally devouring the Knowledge in that book. One of my biggest desires still is to be able to meet this author. Her experience and teaching had saved my life (I made contact, via the internet, with the author, thanked her, and she replied, Halleluja)

But over all of this, the Love of Jesus and the Father for this inexperienced and uneducated daughter of His, still towers above everything else,

Therefore Psalm 18 verse 35 says: "HE TEACHES MY ARMS TO DO WAR" (Naturally, of course, the evil spirits in the atmosphere around us.)

I hide the book at home, underneath other books, because now the enemy was furious; because his deeds were, brought into the Light of Jesus. Also, by my bedside, I have a lot of books about the second coming of Jesus Christ, as well as my various Bibles.

The children were in the habit, as they were doing years before, to utilise our shower. The boy, walking through our room, he dashed to my bedside and glared angrily at the book I was busy reading, about the second coming of the Lord. It had been one of the books, I had brought from the farm attic. I didn't pay any heed to his weird behaviour and the disgruntled look on his face about my reading material. I continued reading while he proceeded to take his shower.

The next day I received an urgent phone call from the housecleaner: "Madam, you were right, this boy most certainly must be involved in satanism!" She sounded very anxious. "I just heard a loud noise coming from your bedroom and when I got there, he was throwing books around and your bibles, he was swearing at the Lord who killed his mother and the Lord that Madam is serving." Astonished, I listened to the confirmation. "Oh, I had such a fright, and I told him, although I am not a devout Christian, he cannot swear at the Lord like that! I saw my very rich uncle stand in front of the church door and do that, swearing to the Lord, and after that he lost everything and died, as a poor beggar on the streets. I told the boy that.!" (Yes, reader, those were her very words to me. And not two weeks after this incident, the boy lost a very good job and for a very long time after that, he could not find work again.)

Just a few hours after that phone call, a Christian colleague of mine, gave me a Biblical diary. I opened it right away, on that day's date. Ecclesiastes 10 verse 1: As dead flies give perfume a bad smell, so a little folly outweighs wisdom and honour "

I saw the Light! The evil powers within him, are like flies in ointment.

Now I understood why nothing good could come to pass, why there was continuous unhappiness and bickering in my marriage. Those evil powers are making the ointment, which was meant to give off a pleasant smell, stink to high heavens.

That evening, I stood in front of my closet. Remember, earlier I mentioned something about the truth which I had discovered...I was talking, my words were stopped, I couldn't speak, as my husband grabbed me and threw me onto the bed, pinning me down with his knees, his hands around my neck to start suffocating me. His eyes looked cruel, as I had never seen them before. It wasn't even him; he was so strong, and his eyes looked hard and evil. The thought shot through my mind, that it must be those demons from the son, which were now working through my husband. He shouted: "Tonight I will kill you!" I saw the Evil one wanted me dead. Softly I got , through my lips: "in Jesus' Name, in Jesus' name!" All of a sudden, his grip loosened, and he let me go. I heard him talk loudly and said: "this God had thought he would get me down with the death of my wife; He will not succeed; I'll show Him!"

I was totally lame with fright; I knew I was on a different level of my life and there would be no turning back. Dr Rebecca Brown's book teach, if the devil manifests through people, that person wouldn't remember anything of the incident. The next day I had a conversation with him, he didn't know anything about it. "You tell lies very easily! Why would I do and say such things?!" Then I understood... it was evil spirits, and he was being used as conductor to do their deeds.

That was my first experience and lesson in these things. The devil hates the Truth.

John 14 verse 6: "Jesus answered, I am the way and the TRUTH and the life. No one comes to the Father except through me."

Little did I know of which and how many things I would still learn in the future; sometimes through my own mistakes and sometimes through wisdom. It became clear to me that I would have to reach out for Spiritual guidance and help from true believers who know the Might of the Lord and would be able to pray and fight with me.

The next day a colleague, to whom I sometimes had chatted with about this situation, approached me at work, with this request: "Could our church members not come and have a prayer meeting in your house?"

I asked the Lord: "Master, I do not know these people, please make it clear for me, if they would be the right Spiritual warriors for me?"

1 Chronicles 12 verse 17: "David went out to meet them and said to them, 'If you have come to me in peace to help me, I am ready for you to join me. But if you have come to betray me to my enemies when my hands are free from violence, may the God of our ancestors see it and judge you.'

verse 18 Then the Spirit came on Amasai, chief of the Thirty, and he said:

'We are yours, David!
We are with you, son of Jesse! Success, success to you,
and success to those who help you, for your God will help you.'
So, David received them and made them leaders of his raiding bands."

So here I had brave fighters coming to my aid. "Thank you so much, Father, I know it is You sending them out to me!" Eagerly I invited them to do it, but we decided it would need to be done in secret. We decided, on a day when I would have the day off work and no one else would be home. Once again, I heard car doors banging and I went out to invite people whom I have never met, into my home, but I felt only peace and love, surrounding me. In awe I watched them get out of a van with a canopy on the back; my tears were flowing for the help the Lord my Father has sent me and I knew, there would be no devil whom they would bend their knees to. They knew Christ and His risen Power. My whole life-pattern would change from that day onward, to this day, now 23 years later, I had once again begun anew. There were many, may be eight, ten-people, my need was so great!

First, they prayed for me. One of the sisters in the Lord sat in front of me on her knees and clothed me with the full shield of faith as described in the book of Ephesians;

Ephesians 6 verse 11;" Put on the whole armour of God, that you may be able to stand firm against the schemes of the devil.

She made all the movements over me; the helm of His redemption over my head and the breast shield she pulled over my chest, by more hand movements she pointed out the belt of truth around my waist, she waved over my feet to put the shoes of Peace of the Evangelism onto my feet. She lifted my left hand and pointed out how she put the shield of faith into my hand and with another wave of her own hand, she placed the sword of The Word into my right hand. I felt the Power and Peace flush over me. At that point in time, my life, had been one big ball of nerves, because I didn't have the knowledge of how to fight this enemy. I didn't know about, or the power it had.

As one of the sisters in the Lord had put it: "It is like a boxing match; the devil thought he had knocked you out, he had already counted to nine-and-a-half, when Jesus entered through us, and knocked him out; and now you are getting up, to fight once again!" Oh, and were those true words spoken!

They walked from room to room and called the Power of Jesus Blood, covering, the curtains, the beds, the atmosphere. Never had I known to pray "Lord, change the atmosphere". Because they were praying quite loudly, and they were a different nation than myself, a neighbour came knocking on the door to see if everything was alright. I told him all was in order, that we were merely praying. Then he disappeared again.

They went to the cleaning girl's, bedroom and begged her to give Jesus Christ a chance in her life. She acknowledged that she would do it, but at a later stage... They warned her that Jesus had given her a chance on that day and that she might be denying His Grace which could later prove to be too late...

(Truthfully, a few months onward she absconded from work and a while after that I noticed that she had become a street-person, sleeping on the streets, and pushing a trolley around. I had spoken to her again about Jesus reaching out to her, but she did not take heed.)

That night, peace dawned over the house! To my astonishment, I saw the daughter was reading, the bible my parents had given her. That is the Power of what their prayers in the name of Jesus had brought about in our house. Truly our fight is not one of flesh and blood, BUT AGAINST THE POWERS AND SPIRITS AND REGIMES AND STRONGHOLDS IN THE AIR.

(Reader, every child of Jesus should go in prayer, through every room of their house, to experience this salvation, the children, cannot pray for themselves, we have to intervene and pray for their salvation.)

4. SISTER HOPE ARRIVES…

There was especially one sister in the prayer group, sixty years old, who continually caught my attention. I asked her if I may call " Therefore, since we are receiving a Kingdom that cannot be shaken, let us be thankful, and so worship God acceptably with reverence and awe,

Verse 29 for our "God is a consuming fire."

I did not know my Master, but now I realised His character was not known to me. The Holy Fear of the Lord I did not know. In the days of Noah, the Lord regretted creating mankind due to the continuous evil thoughts of His creation. To return to Jesus would wash away my sins, but that would be only the start of the journey, I suddenly realised. Now I still had to be redeemed of a whole lot of my sinful habits. But above all I had to really learn His Will for each moment of my life.

I made a very sincere and important decision, from the depth of my being; I wanted to learn to know the heart of my Abba Father. I had learnt a great lesson through His discipline and from Him withdrawing His Hand from me in punishment. I tasted that consuming fire. Yet, it was still within His great love. The heartbreak and the pain that I suffered (brought unto myself through my disobedience), was now working to the good of my salvation, in His kingdom.

Never before had I been this sincere to seek His presence and His power, like I did now. It had made me ready to pay the price, to be able to hang on to this Godliness. As if it would be the most important source for life in me, I realised I could not live a purposeful life if it was not with Him. The "open confession" was a wonderful experience and redemption. They also receive wisdom during the prayer and would intervene with "Sister also seeks forgiveness for this or that" as revealed to them.

As I was praying and confessing my sins, they would pray: "Lord, put it under Jesus Christ, Blood and wash it away". They also told me that, after this, we would not speak of any of it again, but I would be walking forward, a free being.

5. FRIENDSHIP AND HAPPINESS…

My friends now desperately wanted to meet Sister Hope, because they could see that she was a part of my life. So, I organised for a visit, for her and her husband. Her husband was now also with Jesus and sister Hope accepted these friends of mine with love. When this friend, did not understand us from time to time, Sister Hope would explain to her the Godly things very patiently. I was experiencing great Power emanating from Sister Hope as she was talking, almost as if she was a different being; as if respect for her was forced upon you, as if the Lord Himself was here right now.

I realised once again, how much wisdom I still needed before I could assist the newly converted. I was only but one step or two before!

This friend had been married for around 7years. I will never forget the message on their wedding day; around the conversion of water into wine by Jesus. The preacher explained that they were getting married on that specific day, being very much in love, but that was just as the first wine which would inevitably run out, but then you will need a miracle to convert water (the infatuation now over with) into wine. If you turn to Jesus right then, He will do it for you, and He will have saved the best wine for last! That truly became the reality of their marriage; Jesus Christ, walked in, right when the wine had run out and they needed a miracle.

As her husband progressively grew within the stature of Jesus Christ, she regained a lot of love and respect for him. On Mondays he would go out with the Evangelistic team, of his church, working on lost souls in teams on the streets within the Lord's guidance and he would return home very happy… something they have lost along the way.

Truthfully speaking, when you hand your marriage over to Jesus, he will certainly polish those blemished spots into their once shiniest glory; just like a copper pot regaining its former shining glory. We walk the road alongside of them, and we pray together regularly.

After church on Sundays we would go to our house for coffee and further discuss the sermon.My husband ran away, because he feared this new Life, he witnessed amongst us. He had known most of these people before and now could see their changed lives. "Is that lot still there?" he would ask over the phone calling from the club... then I would just reply with a simple yes or no, and he would decide whether, to come home or not.

On one occasion Sister Hope received Word that the brother would receive a white van. At that stage, his van was really old. Once again, truthfully, it had been wisdom directly from the Lord, because the very next week, he received a white van from his employer, to use indefinitely. One week later though, the employer said, the van to be returned. We could not understand this and went into prayer. James 1 verse 6 "But when you ask, you must believe and not doubt, because the one who doubts is like a wave of the sea, blown and tossed by the wind

Verse 7, "That person should not expect to receive anything from the Lord.

Verse 8 "Such a person is double-minded and unstable in all they do."

WHAT THEN, IS PRAYERS IN FAITH? It is slowly revealed to us; if that doubt comes after the prayers, we should pray: "Master, I praise You, for that which I cannot see now." Further, take heed of how you speak; when you have finished praying about a subject, you have to believe: "Master you are fixing this problem already" even while you cannot see anything yet. Also, I concentrate not to keep asking for the same thing over and over again in prayer, because that would mean I do not believe!

Master had heard already the first time when I asked and the process for the resolution was already in motion. Oh, such basic things, yet so powerful.

I also started writing letters to Jesus about my needs. I open His Word and copy that Scripture next to my request. Then I place it under my mattress. It is astonishing to witness how the Father honours faith.

Hebrews 11 verse 6 "And without faith it is impossible to please God, because anyone who comes to Him must believe that He exists and that He rewards those who earnestly seek Him."

I have learnt valuable lessons from the white van issue. I hear Sister

Hope witnesses to the fact that she had been praying for a very important issue. She said these words: "my sister, I entered in prayer for this important case, I have no doubt in my heart, as the Lord has helped me before in very dark times, so will He intervene in this also." She also taught me that doubt is a sin, because the one who doubts, is doubting Abba Father's strength and might. "Yes Lord, please forgive my doubtfulness, wash it away with Your Blood, reconstruct me and grant me the faith You have, in Your Father while You were here on earth. You did not doubt for one second. Amen"

Sister Hope had a gentle, almost child-like way in her dealings with people. It was as if she got right down under and into your problem, lifting you up; never was it as though she was looking down on you or trying to help you from way up there. It makes me think of Jesus on the mountain when he was teaching his disciples.

I also learnt that the Holy Spirit has to lead you according to each person's uniqueness and the circumstances which differ from person to person, in how you have to adjust how you deal with them and what you need to say. Nothing is about you yourself, but it is all about the person and his or her needs. (This is also exactly how Sister Hope lived her life and what she showed the world.)

It is dangerous if you try to work with fellow believers through your own insight, human knowledge, strength and human wisdom.it can bring about great damage and tear people apart. His great Love remains the most important aspect for His souls and His flock. She explained to me the importance of how you address believers and loved ones.

1 Peter 2 verse 17: "Show proper respect to everyone, love the family of believers, fear God, honour the emperor."

1 Peter verse 17 NASB: "Honour all people, love the brotherhood, fear God, honour the king."

1 Peter 2 verse 17, NLT: "Respect everyone, and love your Christian brothers and sisters. Fear God and respect the king."

I learnt to address fellow worshippers as "sister X" or "brother Y". Every time you address a person, you have to refer to them as brother or sister. It is then, that you speak in faith that they will remain your sister or brother IN THE LORD; to remain children of the Kingdom. It really is the language of faith in which you profess over them... the blessings of staying children of the Kingdom.

I started doing this myself and learnt that it was a great truth. To this day, I still address my fellow worshippers as my brother or my sister. We never called each other by our first names. In my former places of worship, I have never heard this but now it became as much a part of me as would be breathing.

A friend whom, I shall just refer to as "J", short for "Jonathan", because we became like David and Jonathan of the Bible. I had known her since primary school and she visits us regularly on our farm, and I too visited regularly at their home.

I had bought my first home when I had been in my early thirties. My father always urged me "Sis, you have to buy a home for yourself. The way you love to travel, you might never get married". I explained to him that I would not qualify for a home loan. A short while later, my father called me and told me to go and ask our matron for a raise. Lest you will have to return and work for the state, where you would be given a home allowance. He explained that he would not be able to take care of me forever. At some point he would have to return to his Heavenly home, that he wanted to be able to do that, with peace in him, I am taken care of.

I got such a fright... how would I ask this of the Matron? But when my dad spoke, I knew that it really was the voice of our Father and that I had to obey. At that point, I had lived and worked only for Jesus Christ my Lord. I was living in Holy Fear of the Lord and in total commitment, very blessed.

As in Matthew 6 verse 32" For the pagans run after all these things, and your heavenly Father knows that you need them.

Verse 33 But seek first his kingdom and His righteousness, and all these things will be given to you as well.

Verse 34 Therefore do not worry about tomorrow, for tomorrow will worry about itself. Each day has enough trouble of its own."

Truly! I am coming from matron's office and I did ask! My legs still felt a little shaky, but she replied with "I will get back to you" and I was out of there.

"Dad, I did ask her! I am waiting for her reply" I babbled as usual over the phone. My parents prayed in full faith and trusted with me. A short while later, I was summoned to matron's office. I was warned... Here is an offer from management, but no one is to know about it! It will be added to your salary; do with it as you find best. We have calculated that, with the "first buyer's discount", you will be able to buy something. The matter is closed. She handed me a piece of paper with an amount written on it; just an insignificant little piece of paper... But it has changed my standard of living immensely. I phoned my parents immediately. "Mom, I got it! The increase which I needed to be able to buy my own home!" My father came to the city and he handled the whole buying process for me. He studied the building plans himself, before we signed. It was in a new complex which was still under construction. My father had not been happy that I would have a corner stand with no entrance from the front. All would have to drive, all the way around, to enter at the back door. It was unacceptable to him, so he went to see the architects and the builders about it. I refused to buy, if that wasn't rectified. Well, to this day, there is an opening in the surrounding wall of that home. I must receive people from the front entrance. I was still a small amount short, my father agreed to sponsor me.I had taken up in-service training,paid for by the state, and received a salary also in those days. (All of my other siblings had gone to study at our father's cost,he felt it fair to spend some money on me,too) And so, it was that I had bought my first home.

In the first week after I had moved in, there was a knock on the door. "Hello, I saw the motor registration is from the country town where I was born.I just had to know who lives here!". As I came closer, the both of us called out in surprise! It was J. So, we picked up where we had left off after all those years of not seeing each other. She told me her marriage wasn't a very happy one. She visits and passionately rambling on, waving her hands in the air; "I speak to the walls, you know, nobody listens!" Then she leaves again, feeling all better.

My life on the other hand, was much more peaceful. It was work, prayers, prayer groups, and then work again...

At some point, J's husband divorced her. She was naturally broken. She showed me a letter which her mother (now already deceased) had written her years before. Her mother advised her that it would be better for her to spend her life with Jesus than to marry. That HE would take care of her. I decided,to place Jesus first as MY FRIEND. Try to keep my lady friends and family close. I just felt that, should my marriage come to an end, I have lost, given up precious time with family and friends, all for a shooting star.

Every free moment I had; I would spend with loved ones who precious to me. All of my friends, were talkers, and our hearts were filled with the sweetness of our Lord Jesus. We made plans... When we would go walking, each would have time to talk until the next corner and then it would be the other one's turn. Or when we would go to, eat out, then one would literally have to put up a hand and say "excuse me, I would like to have a turn to speak when you finished!" in the dark time of difficulty in our marriage, this was a cool oasis in the dry desert.

I had begun living again. I later learnt also that the enemy despised it when the children of God were happy. The enemy of the Cross worked through my husband; I was attacked numerous times with moods of jealousy towards my friendships. My friends came in and out of my home and always treated my husband in a very friendly manner.

I have had many conversations with people, where one spouse had been unfaithful, there would be severe jealousy, because they could not trust themselves. J was a very beautiful woman (she still is) and my husband often accused me, that she is introducing other men to me.

I must admit, of all my friends, she had been the one closest to my heart; we had together been through the bitter and the sweet things in life. We would often visit with her family and also with mine. We really lived into each other's lives: I had my own cup and special food at her house; when my husband would stay out late at the sports club, we would also visit each other happily.

This would be dependent on her friendships, though. She was in quite a long relationship with a man from out of town, so on weeknights we could visit each other but on weekends she would be visiting him.

I was free to talk about the Word and of Jesus to her, but she hadn't yet come to full commitment to the Lord. One evening her minister visited her and asked whether she had given her life to the Lord. She looked over to me and asked: "have I?" "No", I said. "You have not been" born again" as it's ‚in the Scriptures". She accepted it as such.

6. DARK CLOUDS OF DEATH OVER US...

Then the darkest of times broke over our lives. One night I was reading in "He came to set the captives free" of Rebecca Brown, that according to the Word, chances are that when the devil beseech the Lord to take our loved ones, would we still be serving the Lord? Luke 14 verse26;" If anyone comes to me and does not hate father and mother, wife and children, brothers and sisters – yes, even their own life – such a person cannot be my disciple.
Verse 27 And whoever does not carry their cross and follow me cannot be my disciple.
Verse 28 Suppose one of you wants to build a tower. Won't you first sit down and estimate the cost to see if you have enough money to complete it?
Verse 29 For if you lay the foundation and are not able to finish it, everyone who sees it will ridicule you.
Verse 30 saying, 'This person began to build and wasn't able to finish."

I became aware of my parents; I was calling out loud; "No Master, not my mother and father, please, it is impossible!" She quoted the Bible and mentioned that we should become very still and decide whether it would be possible for us to give up everything for Him, because satan petitioned it of Abba Father, like Job. Upset, I closed Rebecca Brown's book. I cannot agree. A few months after that – my mother only 65 years of age, her illness worsened. She underwent light course of chemotherapy for chronic leukaemia, the doctor said"not at all terminal". In an instant, it turned into active cancer and my mother grappled with death.

My friends told me that should one of my parents die, they would not visit me again, because they would not be able to bear seeing me, we were that close to each other.

Sister Hope prayed with me and trusted with me for healing. I wasn't prepared to let go of my mother. In times when my father wasn't with me, I cried uncontrollably; it was as though my whole world was being torn apart. I physically felt the pain of it. By that evening, there had been no turn for the better and mother realised she, would not get better.

She spoke to us, her daughters, the others left the room. I, the youngest, remained in the room. Thank you, Master, for this Godly moment. "Mother, please forgive me for what I had done to you, going into a wrongful marriage (and desertion Jesus). She replied: "Darling, we have forgiven you a long time ago already. We just didn't want for you to grow old, alone. Now, you will have to be very strong and stop crying; you have to take care of and help your father." My tears were falling uncontrollably. That was our last conversation. The next day she died peacefully.

The strength of the Lord descended on me like I have never known before. When the news came, we had been at one of my father's cousins, also a true believer, and I just said, let us pray; mom has gone to heaven. Dad was calm and peaceful.

That morning, filled with faith, I had proclaimed, Dad, today Jesus will heal mom, we all must pray together." My father silently shook, his head and handed me the Bible, opened;

 2 Corinthians 5 verse 1 "For we know that if the earthly tent we live in is destroyed, we have a building from God, an eternal house in heaven, not built by human hands."

Then, with tears streaming over his face, my father softly said: "mother is going to heaven. The Father of the universe had given my father supernatural strength and He spoke into my mother's ear: "my wife, you can go home peacefully, I am alright." Hours later, she passed away.

My father told me that he had never been as close to the Lord as he was then. He quotes Mother Teresa: "If you had not come to that place where Jesus is all you have, then you have not yet come to know Him." That is what my father experienced at the time of my mother's passing. Jesus had now become his all and he received comfort. He stated that, if that is how it is, one should actually have been praying for a time like this to enter your life, as painful as it may seem., Jesus Christ comes down and carries you in His arms… which would be something you would not have known if death had not come to your door. I also received immediate comfort. It was as if something had inexplicably fallen away from me. I was criticised for suppressing my feelings because that was not how my family knew me. But my feelings were quite visible over my face, the deepest comfort which I had received from the Holy Spirit, was a reality. Through it all, Sister Hope was also winding through my life. I called her regularly and we would pray together on the phone. I received great support from her.

Matthew 5 verse 4. "Blessed are those who mourn, for they will be comforted."

That is a promise that we can pray over ourselves from the Lord. My circle of friends all shows their surprise,, with my strength, at this time.

One day, before my mother went to her forever home, J called me, crying uncontrollably. Her boyfriend had been cycling, when he suddenly fell over backwards and died of a heart attack, immediately. They would possibly have married that year. Her life was now shattered. But Jesus comfort carried her in the time of sorrow.

2 Corinthians 1 verse 4 "who comforts us in all our troubles, so that we can comfort those in any trouble with the comfort we ourselves receive from God."

When they are troubled, we will be able to give them the same comfort God has given us. In this time, J also gave her life completely to Jesus and Sister J grew wonderfully in the Word.

Nine months later, my father also went to his Heavenly Father. The Sunday evening, he mentioned to me "Darling, it is becoming too lonely for me." It was as though I heard in his voice that he has already spoken with our Father. The very following Thursday, he walked over, in his sleep, to Jesus… He had come for him. I cried for two days straight; when suddenly that same comfort dawned upon me and I experienced the Heavenly comfort which surpasses all reason, that which cannot be explained.

Your heart is suddenly healed, and you are able to speak of him without that pain and longing. Thank you, Master, for that comfort! Reader, ask the Lord, Abba Father, to also grant you that gift, even if at this point if you know heartache, there is Heavenly comfort, such as no one on earth can give you, no matter how kind they may be to you.

7. STEP BY STEP TO THE BLISS OF SALVATION

Sister Hope shared her experiences of her husband,which passed to his Heavenly home. He converted years after she did, but also served the Lord. She told me what a wonderful man Jesus had made out of him. He had been used by satan many times before his repentance, and had also left her numerous times for other women. Sometimes he would say nothing, but she always knew and stood firm in her faith with her children. She told me they never went hungry because Abba Father was her true husband. Sometimes her husband would burn his weekly wages in front of her eyes, then she would just praise the Lord in knowing that He will provide. She laid the table, with no food. The Children eager to know, where is the food? "The Lord said He cares for the little birds so He will care for us." Nearby neighbours brought cooked meals (they were going to trow it away) from the restaurant, where she works! She put water, salt in the pot,with no food in the house,start cooking as if she had food.The children crying what are we going to eat?Later,knocking on the door. Somebody gave her food for the pot! Many days,we would go for rides together and these testimonies of hers helped me greatly along my way.

One day she told me that shortly after her husband's passing, she had a dream. In the dream she had to cross a bright river; the water was so bright you could see the rocks down under the water. A woman from the same nation as I was standing on the other side and encouraged her to keep walking. When she reached the other side, the woman was there with a white car and asked her to get in and drive. She replied, she didn't know how to drive, but the woman insisted. When she got in, she drove up a very steep mountain. It was really impossible to drive there, but they made it to the top. She told me: "Sister it was you standing there." At that point in time I was driving a white Toyota!! For a few moments, I just sat there... I had no words... slowly it began to sink in... ABBA FATHER had known long before I even started the journey with this mighty warrior of Faith, (mother in the Lord, never had I known such an authoritative figure of Christ, Jesus was literally beaming from her being) and He planned it as such.

That dream was so real!!! Sister Hope had to drive in the Spirit, because I wasn't equipped for the fight against the powers and evil working from within my marriage. As she put it in later years: "I had to crawl before the Lord, fast and pray days and nights without end, to save sister, from dark powers of satan. But the Lord had taught her through His Spirit, to drive out to the top of the mountain, with me beside her. The Father was helping me, by giving unto me a childlike and humble spirit to give,her the wheel , to allow her,to drive me to the top of this seemingly impossible high mountain in the Spirit. I had to come down from my own self-appointed highness, and come under the authority of Jesus Christ within her, to be obedient. Often, I would hear: "Sister, we must die of the self... the self is still standing upright and that is hindering the work of the Master."

The past played itself out in my mind's eye. My father had bought Angora goats, to his predicament. "Oh Darling, I have learnt a lesson from the Father, desire got the better of me, because their wool is very valuable, with everything I have put into it, I am just breaking even. They are very beautiful but are so tender and they die easily. The slightest cold front could hit, and they are gone. Look at this now (we were standing by a small dam) The sheep are walking neatly in a row, drinking from the water, each getting their share, and then they move on in an orderly fashion. These goats, however, are rowdy and bashing one another with their horns. They all land up in the dam until the water is so dirty, and none of them really got some water in the end.

It comes before me: it's like this; if I should ask "oh Lord, please let me experience;

Gal 2 verse 20 "I have been crucified with Christ and I no longer live, but Christ lives in me. The life I now live in the body, I live by faith in the Son of God, who loved me and gave himself for me."

It is an issue of faith... Sometimes you leave food and rather fast and enter into prayer and trust the Lord that I would taste the laying down of the 'self ' or else I would be like the Angora goats with all my limitations and weaknesses and contaminate the pure water from the Lord and render it useless to anybody else. On one occasion, a sister came to visit, Sister Hope for a few days. She irritated me intensely, her way of speaking and doing things, just didn't sit well with me.

One morning I had the strongest desire... "The self, the "own I" within myself, would have to die; like a fire, burning in me, it became more and more urgent and I called out;" Lord let me experience it, Your rising power, alive in me, my own "I"nailed to the cross."As Sister Hope always says, rather be covered in shame here on earth and be saved, than being shamed at Jesus's feet after you die.

That day, when I was at Sister Hope's again and the "irritating" sister was there, (the one that I couldn't wait for to leave, because according to big old me, she wasn't up to standard) I felt such love towards her and my heart went out to her. All at once I saw the great need within her, I helped her. Begins a journey with her, in great love and patience. I experienced great happiness within my heart.

I had a bit of a fright at what just occurred, because she was still speaking in that same "irritating" fashion, but all of a sudden, the irritation fell away, and it became overpowered by love. Then it became clear that self- denial was at work here. Sister Hope said many times "Children of God, it is wonderful to live from self-denial, the more deeply you grow into that, the better life here on earth will be for you.

Philippians 2 verse 13; "FOR IT IS GOD WHO WORKS IN YOU, both to will to act according to HIS PLEASURE"

Sister Hope was called the mouth piece of the Lord; "Loved ones, you must in all sincerity do your best to get rid of your weaknesses. You will not be able to do this by yourself, but fast and pray, and fast only for your weaknesses then you will see how Christ will live within you". Therefore, I was so happy when my colleagues would speak to my face about my weaknesses and how I have improved. As Joyce Meyer says, "I am better than yesterday, not yet there, but there is improvement."

All the Glory to the Holy Spirit who keeps on knocking... until I listen. I thought it my duty to speak in the meetings about everything that was wrong because I stood for justice. Sometimes I stood up against authority for the oppressed. I thought I was doing it for Jesus. Until one day when I arrived at Sister Hope's, who had no knowledge, about my conduct. She said something was brought to her attention and she wanted to share it with me. She said, "you know Sister, as I walk with Jesus within the way of the Lord, how wonderful it is for me to stop fighting, hand over all of my rights to Him, how wonderful to experience how He is fixing things, without me having to so much as open my mouth." I had a fright; I prayed immediately. "Master, see everything." It cut right through me… in other words, I was still fighting from the "self".

What redemption followed in my life after this; to this day, I try to be quiet during meetings and there are so much less "moans and groans" about the injustices in the workplace or in the church… Well every so often, my old spirit tries to get through, but I recognise it and return to Jesus Christ, for salvation of it.

1   Corinthians 15 verse 50: "I declare to you, brothers and sisters, that flesh and blood cannot inherit the kingdom of God, nor does the perishable inherit the imperishable."

My prayer: "Lord, save me from the perishable, which is flesh and blood, that which is human… and not like You it has no value in Your Kingdom. Help me to seek only the values of Your Kingdom… Let Your Kingdom come within me, as it is in Heaven and so also on the earth, glory be to Your name… Amen."

I fully accept the testimony which now was rooted within my heart. Stop fighting! Let the Lord Jesus Christ fight for you, get out of His way. Many times, it had been the Lord's will, though, when I kicked against the things (which I perceived as let downs, when things weren't as I wished them).

Many times, I even blamed the devil! Then, for instance, I would see later that the decision of the manager, had been the Lord. Sister Hope sing; "Surrender, oh sweet rest".

Truly, wonderful it was when He resolved issues, only but last week, I received a phone call from the head of my department, to inform me that I should stay at home the coming Wednesday, because there was too little work and too many people on duty. Just as I started to moan, why me? Why should all the others work? (the hours would have had to be worked back at a later stage!) I surrendered… Thank you, I will stay home" I replied, filled with His peace. I realise it is sister's prayer meeting on Wednesday afternoons, something I hadn't attended in a long time because I didn't have Wednesdays off. This meant that I could attend that week!

When I arrived at the prayer meeting, everyone had been so sincerely happy to have me there. The prayer leader said;" because our sister not being with us for such a long time, she brings the Word and can encourage us today." The Holy Spirit supported me. Later I heard a few sisters witness to the fact that they needed that specific message, that day. To me it was as though I had to be there, for a very specific reason. It was an appointment with the Master; it became a wonderful experience, being able to feel such great upliftment after a prayer meeting. That Saturday, I was on call for the theatre department and I was able to work back the hours… no problem. This is but a small example of how sweat to surrender…

Years ago, I noticed some literature of Siege Oblander, taken under correction, it went something like this: "agree quickly with your adversary".

Mathew 5 verse 25 "Agree with your adversary quickly…"

It was a thin little book, containing a Powerful witness. As I remember it, the author had at the time been a fugitive from her government due to her faith. They had been roaming around and the only way out was by boat. When they arrived at the pick-up point, tired and worn out, they heard that the boat had already left. The next boat would be available in months. Feeling hopeless, they prayed… they couldn't understand why they had to go through this disappointment. This meant that they would have to flee and roam around under very difficult circumstances for another month or even two. When they did get a boat, they learnt that the one they had missed, had perished, with everyone on it!!! This story has also had a tremendous impact on me. The message that she conveyed: "agree quickly, with bad circumstances of your life" referred me once again to the times I fought circumstances , not to my liking, angry at how things had worked out.Unhappy for days on end, but when I quickly decided to surrender, I accepted the disappointment and then peace and joy descended upon me quickly. As someone mentioned: "don't let anything steal your joy".

At a joyful prayer meeting and togetherness, Sister Hope mentioned to me that a true believer no longer has to fight and scold. A true believer has to have the quiet soul of the FATHER. It cut right through me, because when my husband comes in so late, I do not have a quiet spirit. It just showed so much disrespect towards me, coming in at the early hours of the morning. Usually I address this and want to talk it through, but it always led to arguments...

That evening I prayed to the Father: " Your Word says in Romans 6 verse 6 "for we know that our old self was crucified with him so that the body ruled by sin might be done away with, that we should no longer be slaves to sin" I want to experience it, Your Attitude, so that my old being, who scolds and fights, could be crucified." As it gets later and later, I become angry again, then I call to the Master again quoting the Scriptures non- stop. On my inside, there is only anger... Long after midnight, I hear the key in the door, and I call to the Scriptures again. When the door opened, the Master did something great in me. Immeasurable peace over me, I asked him, if he wanted a cup of tea... He looked at me in astonishment; I myself was astonished. It was a turning point, the complete and perfect Work of the Master.

In time to come, when he came late, the Lord granted me His attitude.He asked whether I had met someone else, because,I didn't mind him coming late any longer. Glory be to the Lord!

I have heard about so many ladies who have won their husband's for Jesus, by just showing His Attitude in the most difficult of times. It is difficult, but quite possible, when we desire it with our whole heart.

8. THE KINGDOM IS ALIVE...

Disheartened by all the misunderstandings and the disgruntled attitude of everyone in the household, I take a drive out to Sister Hope. The accusations are milling around in my mind. The cleaning girl complained... She had ironed all the daughter's washing and had hung it in her cupboard, when she became frustrated, threw all on the floor. She told me that the daughter wanted canned food for a project, and she wanted to take some of the luxury items, when she advised her to take the more inexpensive ones, as the luxury items were needed for the household. The girl became so infuriated, she kicked the kitchen door, which then was hanging askew from its hinges. I, trying to be as good as Mother Teresa, felt the girl needed help to rectify her wrongful behaviour. That night my husband once again returned home in the early morning hours from the club. Had I applied wisdom; I should have left it for her to sort it out with my husband. But no, the "old I" intervene. Even before he had had something to eat in the morning (AGAIN, NOT VERY WISE OF ME!) I said," just want you to know the cleaner had complained about..." He yelled down the passage: "Daughter! Did you kick the door?" She replied in an angelic little voice and with an angelic expression on her face: "no daddy, I only closed the door with my foot." And with "Do you see... you only want to cause trouble once again!" he stormed out and off to work. Humiliated, I turned around... case closed... we are wrong, his little lamb is not guilty. Today, I realise that I could have handled things differently.

I was still battling to get over what had happened the previous weekend. Forgiveness had not yet come to my heart. It was his birthday, and we would have gone out together. I waited and waited. Late at night they brought him home, helped him onto the bed and let him lie there, diagonally across the bed. He slept that very deep drunken kind of sleep. That was the "lovely" birthday...I decided, enough is enough and before he woke, I had packed a bag with clothes for the weekend and set off.

I reached the coast, almost two hours' drive from the city and booked myself into a guest house with one purpose in mind: he had to suffer and not know where I am; naturally I had turned my cell phone off.

My thoughts were like a tornado dwelling between divorce or staying... The two owners of the guest house are friends; two ladies whom both were divorced. We had lots of chats and got on very well. Late that evening, the conversation turned to marriage. They must have seen the torment of my face. One of the ladies told us her ex-husband is an alcoholic. Just in time realised he was dragging her down with. She gave me some advice; said that I should grow strong within myself; that I should stand up for myself and protect myself, otherwise that lifestyle would drag me down and keep me bonded. Her advice WISDOM, BUT THE WISDOM OF JESUS CHRIST WORK DIFFERENTLY! (With the help from the Lord, it did not happen. I got pulled down, but like a bottle-cork, always pop back-up, from deep underneath the water, every time. Even when I was pushed down with great force,but as soon as the storm is over, it shoots UPWARDS, AND IT REMAINS ON TOP OF THE TROUBLED WATER.The Lord will guide you, what is right for you. The Good Shepherd lifted me up,every time,at work or a blessing that is so big,that people became so jealous.I learned, not to share all of my blessings.

I picked up a very special shell, that weekend, I had it framed and hanged, on my bedroom wall, so that I would REMEMBER THE SOLUTION of that weekend... "TAKE CARE OF YOURSELF". Untill today,I go out,in nature and treat myself a lot,it give me balance,and strength to go on.

The words of Sister Hope's pastor rang in my ears: "Sister, the Lord always has a solution, for any marriage, we do believe in SEPARATION." He did not know about my circumstances and thus that message he would have gotten from the Father Himself. My Heavenly Father knew when I needed some "separation time".

By Monday I switched on my cell phone. It was actually so lovely while I had it off... Shortly, my husband called. He apologised as always; he explained the guys would not let him go, that they had mixed his drinks. Yes, it could be the truth, he didn't often get so severely drunk. He sounded really sorry, but I was not ready to forgive. On my way back I first visited, Sister Hope's and we prayed together. She encouraged me to forgive and insisted that the Lord could still change him. While she was holding my face lovingly with her two hands, she asked "Sister, do you believe that the Lord can change him?" I replied, "No sister, I cannot see that happening". She replied "well, I believe it without a doubt... I witnessed my own husband change from an angry lion into a meek little lamb in Jesus Christ." So, I drove away from there, with divorce still an option in my mind. Later I learnt that Sister Hope and other prayer buddies had fasted and prayed for three days "because if the sister should get divorced, she might make the same mistake and remarry the wrong person again". They moved my heart in His Wisdom. Once again, confirms that dream... Sister Hope drove my car up the mountain. As the Word mentions in Mark 9 verse 29: "He replied, 'This kind can come out only by fasting and prayer."

And so, a divorce started flowing out of my mind and my being like a stream of water, away and away... until it became so thin and weak and later totally had dried up.

But soon I was amidst a big storm again... Only a week later, I was in my car again, going to Sister Hope to throw out the whole bag of potatoes. It had become too much for me to carry... Sister Hope is always very happy to see me. The Father had put abundant love for me into her heart. She clapped her hands and exclaimed "Am I happy today about the husband in Sister's life!" I was astounded; was he now going to convert and turn to the Lord; would we soon be worshipping Jesus together? It was all I could think of... She went on to say: "If it wasn't for him, Sister would not been driven out to me! Seek Jesus, with your whole heart; what a miracle, sister you are totally dependent on His solution today. Now, Jesus Christ Himself can make something right in your life. That is SOMETHING you have never been able to allow Him, your total surrender." ... 'Have Your Way oh Lord' With that, the wind was taken from my sails. It is not what I had wanted to hear!!! Everything that I wanted to complain about, was gone!!! We prayed and had a peaceful cup of tea together. She would sometimes keep something she had made for me "I specially kept this piece of Sago pudding for you. I knew you would enjoy it..."

The little things... True love was healing me. Sometimes we would drive out to the sea or to beautiful places in nature and we would enjoy our time together in the Lord's presence.

Renewed and filled with courage I drive home. Before I go, she would pray "Sister, I have to put you on the road". This specific prayer was very precious to me: "Lord, we pray in Jesus' Name now that every single evil spirit awaiting her return, at sister's home, be powerless, in the name of Jesus Christ." I had also learnt, how to pray through our home and with my fingertips in oil, touch everywhere, in His Mighty Name.

Ephesians 6 verse 10; "Finally,be strong in the Lord and in His mighty Power.

Verse 11 Put on the full armour of God, so that you can take your stand against the devil's schemes

verse12 For our struggle is not against flesh and blood, but against the rulers, against the authorities, against the powers of this dark world and against the spiritual forces of evil in the heavenly realms."

Become mighty in this process!! I had grown by taking small steps at a time. Sister Hope has grown a lot over the years in His power and became mightier, against these forces of darkness. I was still like a baby. I had known nothing of this or how to wage war against evil in His name.

1 Samuel 1 verse 37: "The Lord who rescued me from the paw of the lion and the paw of the bear will rescue me from the hand of this Philistine."

Saul said to David, "Go, and the Lord be with you."

The lesson I had taken from this was that David also had to grow and found his teaching in nature, with the lion and the bear... There he also grew mightily in the Lord. Now he was able to slay the giant Goliath and so save the nation. Just as Sister Hope now was saving me within the Lord...

At that stage I had still been a bundle of nerves. Sometimes my pulse reach,120 beats per minute when I arrived at work. Nothing in my being could handle the rude behaviour in that house. We were raised very gently. Therefore, I became, very desperate for a solution from the Lord. It was as though the Master, in His wisdom,thought "I am giving her over to her own desire to have this man, so that her heart will return to me."

Today I can declare that I am thankful for that muddy road that I had to travel; the uphill stretches that made me search for Jesus in total sincerity.

Romans 8 verse 28, NIV: "And we know that in all things God works for the good of those who love him, who have been called according to his purpose."

Even my misconceptions, my mistakes, wrongful actions, and disobedience would bring me answers and solutions; not as I had wanted it, but to enter through the narrow gate which leads to eternal life.

As you, who read here might see, my search was for love and acceptance from my husband, I wanted to experience his love for me. I longed for him to make me happy. That is how I left the road at point A in my life. I had travelled a wonderful road with Jesus Christ, but then I started craving the love of a human husband and a child. This is what hurt my Father's Heart. Just like I was hurting now… ABBA FATHER had sent His son so that I would return into Friendship and Oneness with Him, like Adam and Eve had been, before their fall from Grace.

How much pain would have been averted for myself and many of my dearest ones, had we not placed such expectations on our workplace or husbands or wives or children! We wanted those expectations to fill us with that deepest of happiness and companionship. The blood of Jesus Christ THE LORD has flown, to buy me BACK as one of his personal friends.

Romans 5 verse 10 (Good News Edition) "We were God's enemies, but He made us His Friends through the death of His Son. Now that we are God's friends, how much more will be saved by Christ Jesus.

Verse 11 But that is not all; we rejoice because of what God has done through our Lord Jesus Christ, HE MADE US GODS' FRIENDS."

Once again, divorce was not the solution, for me. The Master was in the process of changing me, to His Likeness. I would have missed out on many valuable lessons, had I left my marriage at that point… Yes, it did make my life much more difficult, but the Hand of Abba Father, which produces lot of miracles, I would have missed. Despite everything, I can give so many testimonies which can aid many loved-ones of the Lord and encourage them, like I had been helped and encouraged. That is why I am writing here. Because I followed His, my Shepherd's voice, I was given many blessings.

John 10 verse 4 "When he has brought out all his own, he goes on ahead of them, and his sheep follow him because they know His voice."

The strange voices shouted: "divorce him; he will never change" but the gentle voice never said that! Many days I prayed "Master, if my 'own self ' as in Gal.2 verse 20, had died on the cross, what choice will I make at this crossroad?" or, "Master if You had still been here on earth, in my body, what would You have done now?" The Lord hears each and every prayer! I kept an empty shoe box in my locker at work. In it I put the letters I would write to Jesus every day: requests; or how I felt; what I needed; how I would like Abba Father to bring solutions to problems. The letters were like letters from one friend to another.The solutions,as the Father would have it, not always like I would have wanted it. ABBA Father truly became my best friend. Sometimes it would be better for me to go to Him in silence, instead of making conversation with other people.

Never was I tested beyond my strength. The Shepherd would carry me in His arms through difficulty.

1 Corinthians 10 verse 13, NIV: "No temptation has overtaken you except what is common to mankind. And God is faithful; he will not let you be tempted beyond what you can bear. But when you are tempted, he will also provide a way out so that you can endure it."

Many times, I would be given Word:

Matthew 2 verse13 "When they had gone, an angel of the Lord appeared to Joseph in a dream. 'Get up,' he said, 'take the child and his mother and escape to Egypt. Stay there until I tell you, for Herod is going to search for the child to kill him."

The Good Shepherd had, along with temptation, opened so many doors, because the dark forces had tried cruelly, to kill the life of Jesuswithin me. They wanted me to become so forsaken and tired, that I would let go of Jesus, but there would always be help on the way. I sometimes went out with Sister Hope and her church members,on outreaches in the community and other times I went on wonderful holidays alone, even went abroad a few times. My husband got cheaper flight rates through his work, which he never used, but I did! The travels are actually a story all on its own... how blessed I am in this friendship with Jesus. At some point I had prayed: "oh Master, please forgive me, I did put people before You,Teach me, what it is to have friendship with

You. I don't want to feel so neglected any longer by my earthly husband. I want to experience Your love and Your friendship, Master. You hear Sister Hope call You her everything, that she is in love with You. Please bring me also to that point." That prayer has been answered, to this day I am growing in it; deeper and deeper in His love. There were times when I had to flee out of certain situations, and when I returned, the solution was so much better than what I could achieve on my own.

Ezekiel 39 verse 11[Good News Edition] "The Lord said; When all this happens, I will give Gog a burial-ground there in Israel, IN TRAVELLERS VALLEY...

Verse15 they will put or build a marker beside it"

My going away or travels were always serving as beacons in the valley of travellers, as signs of which plans that the enemy had made to destroy Christ in me.

It was overpowered by The Master,every time.The victory in Ezekiel was so great, they took seven months just to bury the enemy. The Master buried a lot of my "troubles" the same way(I do realise this scripture is about the end times in Israel,but so appropriate!). Every journey or time away from home, was witness to God's favour and help in dark times. Yes, I certainly could not just sit back and moan about everything that was wrong, I had to move, as the Shepherd led me.

Genesis 35 verse 7 "There he built and altar, and called the place El-Bethel because there God has revealed Himself to him when he escaped from his brother."

Sometimes, while I was feeling "broken on the inside" I would go with Sister Hope to loved ones. "Sister, today you can encourage us, with your testimony and from the Word. The Holy Spirit is helping you mightily, when you get up from there, even when you are broken and empty on   the inside." I could tell them of my hard times and how the Lord would always resolve situations for me. The solution usually also spills over, encourages others who are in the same situation.When I would get home, something which had been amiss, huge or small, would be resolved. I have found that when I give anything... even if it may be just a glass of water, or a word of comfort and encouragement to His flock, His sheep, Jesus Christ would intervene and resolve issues of my own. I have learnt , a case of "giving". I cannot sit down and stay cooped up in a bundle. The spiritual reborn baby inside me will die. There would be no joy or happiness if I remained stuck with my own problem, I heard Sister Hope say, when she was finished with her homework. She was at home full time. "Master, point me to someone whom I can go out to and tell about how Great You are, or that You love them." Then she would leave her house and she would always meet someone out there who was suffering great need and whom Jesus wanted to help. I bought from a Christian bookstore,"the wheat kernels" with Scripture, both sides. I asked for the Holy Spirit to lead me and I would hand it out where I thought it was needed. The Scriptures would lay the foundation for forthcoming conversation and in that way, I have been able to serve many people in need, with His Holy power. Even if it may prove very difficult; continue to sow, you, the shower of the Good Seed for Jesus.

9. LESSONS LEARNT FROM HISTORY…

At times I would pray together with a lady friend; let's refer to her as "Nr. 3". On one occasion, Nr. 3 came barging in and I could see that she was terribly upset. She was also caught in a very difficult marriage. She uttered these words: "Father, when will my husband's soul come to salvation? You can see that I cannot take it any longer!" She threw her hands in the air, very frustrated with her circumstances.Sometimes we feel like that; but even when she had left, I still felt frightened, because this outburst upset me greatly. Every person has his or her unique relationship with the Lord, but this had been like anger against the Lord… I mean this with great respect to the Lord but it was like she demanded: "Lord, You WILL resolve this issue NOW, and You will resolve it in THIS way; my husband will come to salvation right now and that is that. I will not stand for any nonsense any longer!" As if it the Lord's fault that she had to suffer in that way.

I went to pray,asked the Holy Spirit to explain what I had witnessed.

Numbers 20 verse 8 "Take the staff, and you and your brother Aaron gather the assembly together. SPEAK to that rock before their eyes and it will pour out its water. You will bring water out of the rock for the community so they and their livestock can drink

Verse 9 So Moses took the staff from the Lord's presence, just as He commanded him.

Verse 10 He and Aaron gathered the assembly together in front of the rock and Moses said to them, "Listen, you rebel, must we bring you water out of this rock?"

Verse 11 So Moses lifted up his hand and struck the rock twice with his rod;and water came forth abundantly,…

Verse 12 But the lord said to Moses and Aaron,"Because you have not believed Me,to trust Me as Holy in the sight of the sons of Israel,THEREFORE YOU SHALL NOT BRING THIS ASSEMBLY INTO THE LAND WHICH I HAVE GIVEN THEM

"Oh Master, help!" Sometimes I look just like this… Filled with anger and lamentation… (my version and experience). Moses had at that point also been very tired of the people's continuous moaning. Out of anger, he hit the rock twice, All, God told him to do, was to speak to the rock! That mistake had caused him not to be able to enter the promised land and could only look down from Mount Nebo. The promised green land filled with milk and honey... only observed from a distance...

The lesson for me was if I remain full of anger, the Lord will provide water, but I may never receive the full wonder of His Promise, to the solution of a problem. To this day, I still take heed not to take that attitude; I have failed a good-few-tests in this way; when I became frustrated with circumstances. I pick up the staff and want to hit twice, out of anger, then I would envision Moses sitting on the mountain, without the privilege of entering the Promised Land.

Then I only ask for Grace; "forgive me, Father, for my anger and impatience in this bad situation. Grant me a tender spirit to speak to the rock in faith ' rock', give us water' and from this hard rock, water can now flow, which will comfort me and give me strength, even when things may seem impossible." When there is no well for water, the rock will bring forth water.

On one of our anniversaries, I asked the Lord in the morning " Lord, what do you say on this day about our marriage; to me it appears as a shameful issue?" Every year I would receive expensive gifts and words of appreciation, which was something beautiful, but nothing ever changed for the better.

Hebrew 12 verse 2 "fixing our eyes on Jesus, the pioneer and prefecter of faith. For the joy set before Him He endured the cross, scorning its shame, and sat down at the right hand of the throne of God." In another translation it is written: "which did not deem the shame of the Cross too high; which waited for the Glory".

The shameful situations which had been so many in my marriage, I dare not deem "too high" because as Jesus entered heaven, great things were also awaiting me. At that point I believed it would be the salvation of his soul which would be my future glory; but now, after twenty-four years of marriage, I have yet to see the salvation of his soul. I cannot continually be on the lookout for when he would be redeemed; for then things would be wonderful; no... no... I have to keep my eyes on Jesus, who did not deem the shame of the Cross higher than the Glory which was waiting on Him in Heaven.

As I was holding on to the Help from the Lord every day, I was starting , tasting that Glory of a Heavenly life, although I am living a much more peaceful life now. The Master had thrown so many mountains which hindered me over the years, into the sea.

10. UP A VERY STEEP MOUNTAIN…

At this point, the daughter was full steam into her teenage hood. Her emotions would be sky high just to be very low the next moment. Sometimes she would be low, even down on the ground, for days on end, and then they would suddenly sky rocket again.

Before my wedding, a family member and I spend some time together. She tried to convince me, not to go ahead with the wedding. She is a social worker and has been taught and seen many things. She told me that teenagers could become really cruel during that phase of their lives. This was the area they, as social workers encountered most of their troubles in foster care. Everything would be all well, until that foster child, decides "you are not my real parent" and then any authority would cause problems and rebellion in such a child.

Those were true words and of great wisdom. Now, this was playing out in my marriage. We did have open conversations about her mother and how she had been longing for her. She must have been about 15, at the time. Before then, there had been much less of this missing fase.I explained to her that it was quite normal.

She started going out a lot over weekends. Sometimes, with her head in my lap, she asks for prayer. Other times, she would be too big for that… She would come and ask for prayer, when her troubles had already been huge, and her father not aware.

Our relationship reached its lowest point.From my side, I couldn't believe a word she was saying any longer. She was leading a double life… For our eyes, this one and away from us, the other… Within myself, I was holding back a lot, because I could also not trust her father, or, in different words, I had no confidence in his fidelity. I could carry on with her only to a certain point, because her father could any moment decide against me and in her favour.

This, the risk of being hurt, made me sometimes close up entirely. She had the advantage because he was always in her corner. It was as if they joined into a combined hatred for me.

There came a day, whilst I was visiting friends, with her as well, that someone mentioned to me that she had been seen smoking weed,there. I was so ignorant, made the big mistake in telling this to our house cleaner. The poor woman, she was everyone's adviser. The children talked to her, I sometimes complained to her, my husband also sought answers from her . She had really been the missing link in the chain… or really, the mother of the household. She had been really at home within the household and provided company to the girl when she came home from school; the house was empty then, we weren't around. She asked her "So are you smoking weed now?" At that point of time in my life, my own mother had already gone to heaven and my father and I had been on a tour with a group to Namibia, something dad had always desired. After a lovely tour, I returned home… still head in the clouds… we had time for so many wonderful spiritual conversations and we prayed together every day while we were viewing some of the most wondrous places. My father had apparently been talking and talking to my sister until late at night… in great excitement. I was still in those clouds when I opened the front door.. I did not pray; "Master, cut off the powers of the evil awaiting me!" I was coldly greeted. His lips were pressed together tightly… He didn't even really want to look at me. Later, I heard him mumble "Yes, you only want to cause trouble". Then his tone of voice was raised and the anger flooded from his lips… "Poor child" now she was in such trouble, all because of my talking about her smoking weed, and the police major was involved, a flood of accusations was flung at me. As always,I would only hear: "YOU are bad; YOU are bad!" Although he didn't say it directly, that is how I perceived it. I have to get out of here… is all that was milling in my mind… My bags, not been unpacked and my shift starts at 1pm. With my bags in my car and my pulse racing, I drove to work. While driving, my father called me on my cell phone "Hello Darling, I just wanted to hear how you are?" Oh, his loving voice, it just made the walls come down and my tears were flowing. "Daddy, I still have all of my bags in the car," I sobbed. "I cannot any longer… I am being blamed for everything" Sob… sob… My wonderful father then said "Darling, go to work, park at the security section, your belongings will be save there. You go and work." I know I had gone to a friend with my baggage, to ask for help. She said: "My friend, I do not mind you sleeping over, but your husband will blame me, if you always come over here when you have trouble at home."

Then the whole story unfolded, when the girl realised she had been seen smoking weed, she started a rumour that it had been friend Nr 3's son's girlfriend, who had been smoking weed on that occasion. Unfortunately for her, she had chosen the wrong girl to blame, because that girl's father was a police major, who then told her father, the biggest trouble followed. Now the law was involved, and the major had been to the school . Legal action about smoking weed was in pursuit also. AND IT WAS ALL BLAMED ON ME. I had caused all this trouble... Well, as the saying goes, every struggle has it's sell-by date... Somehow the wind died down and I went home... where there was some kind of forgiveness.

My father called me and said: "Darling, it will be the last time I would ever pray for you about these things, you are wearing me down. I however, got my answer from the Lord... half of the egg is better than an empty shell.So, stay in your marriage". That was the last time, father died a few months later. So why is this horror a part of my story? It became a huge turning point and a great source of help for me in later years. The girl who had been accused, had led a peaceful and steady life, but all of a sudden broke loose and went to England, where she became involved with drugs. We pray for her often... friend Nr3 and I. We trust the Master would lead her back to her old self.

As rivers of blessings flowed upon me, I went to England for a six week hospital-project... away from all the tension for a while... There, I took a trip to Scotland. That Sunday morning, I reached another milestone in my travel journal. We were traveling through Skype, in the North of the Scottish Highlands. I found myself amongst strangers, who were taking the tour with me. Very clearly, the thought entered my mind, that the reason why that girl had turned so bad, was due to my husband's daughter who had put a curse on her!

Softly, I prayed/spoke to the Lord: "Father, it is so good of You to talk to me; but what can I do about it? It has happened, and the curse must have worked, because the girl's life was in shambles."

I was given Galatians 3 verse13, NIV: "Christ redeemed us from the curse of the law by becoming a curse for us, for it is written: 'Cursed is everyone who is hung on a pole. When he was hung on the cross, he took upon himself the curse for our wrongdoing." (I had my Bible with me. While this was my personal experience and not a theological explanation.) I still,did not understand it. As only the Holy Spirit is able to bring us to Wisdom, the picture gradually became clear to me. Just as Jesus had carried the burden of my sins, so did He carry every curse as well! I sat there speechless; over the wonder of this revelation I was given in this little bus. I started praying: "Dearest Master, You had carried every curse. Now I lay that cross over the girl's mouth, cancel that curse, render it powerless against the other girl. Bless the daughter, because she knows not what she is doing, Amen."

We had stopped at a little eatery and eaten some well-known Scottish delicacy named "Haggis". There I made use of a public phone and called friend Nr.3: "Let us quickly pray together in Jesus' name". I informed her of the wisdom that was opened for me and she perceived it the same way as I did. We prayed together, united in our faith, all the way from Scotland right to Cape Town. About a month later, Nr.3 called me to say "that girl had come home like the Prodigal Son!! She is her old self again… She stopped, all of her wrongful behaviours.". I used this lesson. I have learnt in this, many times later, when I needed it. He truly had broken all the curses which had been cast on my family, out of jealousy, envy, hatred, from evil tongues and which came from wrong sources, He rendered all of it powerless and He poured His blessings over us once more. IT IS WRITTEN AS SUCH…

From a second-hand store in a small country town, I found a book called "Curses and Blessings" (Under advisement) written by Derik Prins. In it I found truthful confirmation of that which I had experienced. I would love to read it again, but I have lost my copy by lending it to someone… Just last week I went out looking for it once more in a large christian bookshop, but seemingly it had gone out of print.Likely I found lots of his teaching,as He received it from our Father,on internet.The WORD and the Holy Spirit remain my biggest Teachers, although I do find benefit from other teachers, ONE SPIRIT AND ONE BODY, here on earth as well.

In 2016 I found new literature titled "UNBROKEN CURSES" by Rebecca Brown. I found many most valuable teachings on redemption. It confirms what is written in the Word over and over… The TRUTH, HE had carried all curses to redeem each and every faithful follower. How sweet is that redemption… Sometimes,you will find immediate healing from an ailment, or melancholy which would disappear in an instant. His Joy can return, with a single prayer said in faith and true expectation: "Jesus Lord, our Christ; I now place your cross onto every mouth which knowingly or unknowingly had cast a curse upon me, also, that which I might have knowingly or unknowingly spoken; I cancel it now according to Your Word. Amen." If I remember correctly, Derick Prins wrote (he already with the Lord) if believers become angry with one another, it becomes dangerous arrows; it can be deadly and one might become seriously ill if you don't cut it off in Jesus' name. PRAYER CAN TURN INTO CURSES, WITH EVIL POWERS BEHIND IT AND

BECOME FIERY ARROWS... This I have personally experienced. I have heard faithful people speak of "counter prayers"... when a prayer is said with anger at heart; " Master, teach that guy a lesson or I hand that one into Your Hands now, punish him" I have learnt through my own mistakes, that was not the Love of Jesus Christ. The Scriptures put it clearly:

Matthew 5 verse 44 "But I tell you, love your enemies and pray for those who persecute you".

"Yes, Master, I am also guilty of this... I become angry and even with my thoughts I shoot arrows, sometimes even whilst on my knees. Please forgive me and turn the curses into blessings. Cleanse me with Your Blood of forgiveness and restore me in Your Love... Amen." This I have to pray over and over again, for that imperfection within myself.

There was one occasion where I witnessed this with my own eyes. Sister Hope was very ill when I arrived. She was lying in bed very weak. Suddenly she whispered: "Sister, cut the counter prayers and hostile arrows of X off in Jesus' name." I said another short prayer and asked the Lord to cut it off in the name of Jesus. She whimpered "Amen" and I acknowledged. The next moment she threw off the blankets and got up, filled with strength. When Jesus had cut off that prayer, or those ill-wishes, or gossip, which actually was a curse, the ailment disappeared instantly!!! The Father had shown her, the person, who this, had been coming from. Now, here is the great test; will you be able to pray within His Love for that person? Sometimes that person might not even be aware that he is doing wrong and only our loving prayers can save that person, I learnt from this. "Sister, if we did not pray, on your weaknesses in the past, you also would not have changed.." We always, before we part, have to pray for every person whose name we mentioned in our conversation." When we recognise weakness in others and we do not pray for them, they will never change, and we would be guilty for it." These are invaluable life lessons: "Sister do you know, each morning I wake in the same mood, joyful and in good spirit. The Lord had taught me that it is one of His Gifts to me. The reason for my good mood every day is that I know I have to pray every morning for others who have troublesome personalities and are in difficult circumstances… they cannot help themselves. Most of the time they do not want to be like that… my prayers can help them through the Holy Spirit."

I have failed many tests… I sometimes become angered towards people around me, who can be troubling to me, then I would hear the testimony: "pray for them". Many times, when I shoot up a short prayer, their attitude would change immediately, and they became more friendly and I would find myself in a more supportive atmosphere. Just as they some days also, have to put up with me, it is not as though I behave perfectly every day and, in every way, the Lord Jesus sees everything!

11. HIS BLOOD BREAKS THROUGH EVERY DEEP DARKNESS…

On a peaceful Saturday, Sister Hope and I took a drive out to a dam outside of the city. We order a picnic basket and find a bench amongst beautiful trees. Birds were chirping as if their choir was meant just for us. It was such a lovely atmosphere, a retreat with her was always a blessing for me. It was as though ointment was being applied to the wounds the cruelty of life could sometimes afflict. She began sharing with me: "Sister some of the things I am about to share with you, had never come from my lips, but today I have to share it, on behalf of solutions, also for you yourself." She stated this as plainly as if it was just everyday business. She went on "Sister, you know, before my husband's salvation and redemption, I had to walk a very dark road. On one occasion the Master showed me, in a dream, how a girl was putting something into his drinks, which had come from a sorcerer, who with his evil powers then released evil upon him, so that he would remain with the girl.I prayed and asked Master to render it Powerless through His blood. Honestly, within a few days he returned home, free of that girl. I never spoke to him about it, until after his salvation. I could even describe to him what she looked like."
The Scripture Luke 8 verse 17; "For nothing is hidden that will not become evident, nor anything secret that will not be known and come to light," flashed through my mind.
Never before had I heard the Holy Spirit works like this, but where was this work within my own life, I wondered? She went on: "it was on and off times; he would stay home for long periods and then he would go away again, but I just kept following Jesus… I kept sowing into His Kingdom. My children were little, but we never went to sleep in hunger.There were times,no food in the house,but I trusted the Lord.I start cooking as if there is lots of food.My children ask me what is going in the boiling water and salt?I explained to them, that Jesus said like He cares for the birds,He cares for us.A little later there was a knock on the door,and somebody just had the urge to deliver this parcel,full of what we need.One Sunday morning,I lay the table,with nothing to cook.I had

the hope my Father will not let me down.Later,the neighbour brought cooked food,she works at the airport restaurant, they wanted to get rid of the leftovers.

Sister you know, Jesus Christ is so wonderful, because He knew my husband was going to become one of his children. I was never hurt when he went away like that. One day, I was pregnant, he told me that he was going to another woman. He said he had grown tired of a holy woman. He grabbed his clothes and he crumbled it up into little bundles. I went after him and packed it neatly for him; 'I wouldn't want her to think you have an untidy wife!' Again, I dreamed of the woman with the yellow dress and how fond she was of him.

That was a time in which I had to fast and pray like never before. It was as though that woman had unleashed many powers over him. Many nights I slept on the floor and prayed the whole night through. The baby came too early and I was very ill. The loving Lord did not allow me to die." Her life story engulfed me with great peace, and I realised that she had been prepared to suffer and never wage war.

Her scripture was from 2 Samuel verse 16 "let him curse, for the Lord has told him to. It may be, that the Lord will look upon my misery and restore to me his covenant blessing instead of his curse today."

"Nine months had passed, and I had been very happy in the Lord, without him there. One day, after a prayer meeting, I looked up to the sky and noticed the pigeons flying in a beautiful pattern, the sun was shining through the clouds, it painted a beautiful picture. Suddenly I had a thought... your husband is on his way back to you. I plead with the Lord; I wasn't up to it any longer. Our prayer group prayed together, and the one sister said she had also experienced it as such, that it would be soon. The sister went on to say, when he is back, you may never speak of the past. In desperation I fasted and pleaded with the Lord 'help me, I don't have strength for this any longer'. Again the thought sank deep within myself 'If you take your husband back, it is not as though you are doing him or yourself a favour; you are doing it according to the Father's will. I have to obey my Father. That very same Friday evening, truly, there he stood before me. He asked me to come inside and I opened the door for him; he wanted to go straight to the bedroom. I handed myself over, for the Master knows... should I be assaulted or murdered there, then so be it... that was how I felt. In the bedroom, I was sitting on the bed, he knelt at my legs. Sister, he begged for forgiveness, he was in tears, he confessed every sin possible, everything he had done and everywhere he had been, and said he wanted to serve the Lord from now on. I said, 'yes my husband, I forgive you unconditionally. He informs me, he is just going back for a short time, to take that girl back to her mother, and he would be back the next day. He offered to sleep in the other bedroom, if that was, what I wanted. He just wanted to be back and serve the Lord with his family. He told me how they had often gone to the witch doctor for magic potions, which would cause his wife and the baby to die." He told her the witch doctor had said his wife's faith was very strong, which was the reason she and the baby were still alive. "Yes, my sister, we can say this is nothing; but these are the powers and forces which are mentioned in Ephesians 6. Only the Power of Jesus sustained me... that is why I have had to pray and fast so much. He came back the next day and started following Jesus. The Lord had changed him into such a wonderful man, that people would sometimes come over and stay with us, to witness how the Love of Jesus should work within a marriage.

The day after he came back, we learnt of a terrible bus accident which had happened one week before, in which only one person had died... We were informed, it was the same witch doctor; and yet, here was my husband at home, with a wonderful spirit, totally delivered from this evil. And do you know what sister? I received that spirit from Jesus; I never blamed him for the past; when I said I forgive you unconditionally, truly that is what I did, with my whole heart. I never spoke of it again; it had left my heart and we are walking on a brand new road forward."

The silence stretched out when she had done talking, it was as if words, would have no weight; it would be too worldly to even speak. The Lord's might know no end...

Deep within myself I knew why Sister Hope had to become part of my life. Who else would have been able to teach me about these things? I have never had knowledge of this... I previously had thought of it as nonsense. Now I only saw that if these, undesirable things were somehow ,part of your life, you would have to fight it with the Power of THE LORD JESUS CHRIST.You should seek redemption and salvation. I have heard this before, many times... you cannot go to heaven in a rocking chair; it takes hard work to remain standing in the Faith.

With renewed courage, I drove from there and with renewed testimony, to the fact that the Almighty can do big things. NOTHING, BUT NOTHING, IS TOO BIG FOR HIM. I had taken water from deep within the well of Truth...

With hope in my inner self and my ever-growing faith, one day, I knew, I would also be able to serve people with this Knowledge.

On one of my off days from work, we were going to have a prayer meeting at Sister Hope's and our cleaning girl indicated that she wanted to join us, as well as a colleague. As usual we would first read from the Bible and go on our knees to pray... The PRECIOUS HOLY SPIRIT was there and suddenly Sister Hope stopped praying and said: "Sister, I see a huge yellow peach, a beautiful peach, someone had sent it for your husband,(she was coming from the witch doctors) when he would eat it, his love for you would dry up." There was a moment of total silence and then our cleaner, burst out: "Madam, Madam! I came into your room last Sunday morning, while you and your husband had still been in bed." She said the name of the person who had brought that peach to our home with the message, to give it to my husband. "I felt too embarrassed to say it was for him, so I gave it to both of you to share. It is the truth, that which Sister Hope is speaking of."

2 Corinthians 10 verse 4; The weapons we fight with are not the weapons of the world. On the contrary, they have divine power to demolish strongholds

3 Verse 5; We demolish arguments and every pretension that sets itself up against the knowledge of God, and we take captive every thought to make it obedient to Christ."

Daniel 2 verse 22; "He reveals deep and hidden things; he knows what lies in darkness,
and light dwells with him."

Only the Lord Jesus Christ knew the darkness into which I was now dwelling. I also discovered, just as Joyce Meyer mentioned in one of her programmes, that the only way to knock the devil out with one shot, is to spread your testimony everywhere and help others or even warn them, to save them.

Romans 8 verse 28, NIV: "And we know that in all things God works for the good of those who love him, who have been called according to his purpose."

The only branch I had to hold onto, while I had to go into this milling water, was that I had to get this testimony out there... many, been lacking the knowledge like I did, had to hear it.

Hosea 4 verse 6 "my people are destroyed from lack of knowledge. Because you have rejected knowledge, I also reject you as my priests; because you have ignored the law of your God, I also will ignore your children.

I give thanks for many sweet hours spent in prayer, which had become my very breath. I had heard so many times, without a battle, you will not be able to enter heaven, because it is the battles which force you to look for Jesus. I have also heard, and it is so true, that it is a good battle, because that very battle keeps you close to Him!!

12. THE TABLE HAS BEEN SET BEFORE THE COUNTENANCE OF THE DEVIL...

While dark clouds were once again forming over my marriage, and the peace and harmony have disappeared (through the roof or maybe the windows? But it has certainly disappeared). I just remained by the Master's feet or under His protection and the Word had become a total shield for me. I experience every part of it as so truthful and for each occasion there would be an answer. Many evenings the atmosphere of the house would be so heavy, I would just call up the Word into my thoughts and tranquillity would overcome me. It is as if the Word, for example Ps 23 "The Lord is my Shepherd, I shall not want" acts like a weapon in your thoughts. If unhappiness should enter and try to capture my heart, then I would just repeat in my thoughts: "THE" Lord is my Shepherd. The "LORD" is my Shepherd. The Lord "IS" my Shepherd. The Lord is "MY" Shepherd. The Lord is my "SHEPHERD". By putting the emphasis each time on a different word, it would take on a whole different meaning each time you repeat it and so faith would be restored in my heart.

Nahum 1 verse 7 "The Lord is good, a refuge in times of trouble. He cares for those who trust in him"

The Lord is very patient with me; in all of my failings and triumphs; but He is like that with all of His flock. I find that when I do not hold so tightly onto the Scriptures, I could become panicked in certain situations. I would feel there would be no resolve for that issue; but the Scriptures break all of those bonds. Many days I celebrate huge triumphs in my mind, just by singing "Jesus loves me, this I know, for the Bible tells me so".

There is no place for laziness in this world, if I want to lead a meaningful life. I cannot give in to emotions or earthly feelings. I have to break free constantly, or else a wave of circumstances could sweep me away. Even today, with conditions in a much better state, it takes daily exercise to stay ahead of the enemy. He will use anything to reach havoc if I continue to lap it up... there I go again... I only see darkness... But when I read exhilarating texts out loud or would write it down on paper and read it continuously, then the panic disappears. The right phrase would be, I "blindly" believe it. I have many nights, while we lay asleep on our sides, with his arm around me,I held my finger on the opened Word next to my bed, as if to proclaim: "Master, I am not letting go here, until I find the solution!"

Truly, today, I can testify that no promise from His Word ever came back, empty.

Nahum 1 verse 9 "Whatever they plot against the Lord

he will bring to an end; trouble will not come a second time."

Nahum 1 verse 10 "They will be entangled among thorns and drunk from their wine; they will be consumed like dry stubble."

On one occasion, the house cleaner, came to me anxiously: "Madam, I have to warn you, the children and their father went out together for a meal and he promised them that he would divorce you. Now, when they saw the card in front of your bed which he had given you, written inside, how much he loves you, they are very angry." The above-mentioned text I have been reading for days. Before that message, I had not even been aware of any "entangled" plans against me. So, the Scriptures had conquered the devil's plan every time. He did not divorce me.

After a short break away from home, my husband and I returned, as I entered my bedroom,I immediately felt something was amiss. The bed was untidy, someone had slept here. As I pulled back the duvet, I found the bed full of potato crisp crumbs. It was like in the fable of The Three Bears: "who had sit on my chair?!"

This was the only place up to that point, where I had felt completely safe; my "little corner". I called the daughter into the room and she said "no, it wasn't me". I called the cleaning girl... Of course, she had left it as it was, so that I would see it. "Madam, it is the boy,he entertained a girlfriend with her child,in your room."

Something inside of me snapped. I cannot fight against their hostility any longer. I walked out and got into my car, just drove off... somewhere to catch my breath. I called Sister Hope: " don't you think we could just move into my house and then his children stay on their own in their home?" The daughter was now 18, finishing school. I really didn't feel like going to sleep on that bed, where they must have committed every sin, I could think of... My husband by then had been on early pension, so he was at home all day; when I go to work in the day, he could go over to his house. Sister Hope replied: "Sister you ask him, but only if he agrees, because he remains the Priest of your household and you must remain submissive, as God requires that." So, whatever his answer would be, would be the same as though it was the Lord's. We prayed together and trusted...

Proverbs 21 verse 1 "In the Lord's hand the king's heart is a stream of water that he channels toward all who please him."

That night I asked my husband, could we go and live in my townhouse? To which he replied, "yes, because I cannot stand in the middle between you and the children any longer; the stress of it is getting to me, let's do it." I praised the Master, it was a miracle, his heart was in the Hand of the Master's! The tenants in my house had been a young couple and the agreement on contract was two months, notice to both parties. The man was a young advocate of the law. I went to give them notice. It was the 1st of September. My friend Nr.3 was very upset; she felt the Lord will not operate like that. As I always would do, I went to the Scriptures to get confirmation from the Lord. The Lord is so faithful when I am sincere.

Haggai 2 verse 18 "From this day on, from this twenty-fourth day of the ninth month, give careful thought to the day when the foundation of the Lord's temple was laid. Give careful thought:

Verse 19 Is there yet any seed left in the barn? Until now, the vine and the fig tree, the pomegranate and the olive tree have not borne fruit.

"'From this day on I will bless you."

Verse 20 The word of the Lord came to Haggai a second time on the twenty- fourth day of the month:"

Astonished I sat there; "Dearest Lord, am I hearing this correctly; will I move already by the 24th of September? Is that Your confirmation?"

The next week I went to the tenants, to ask them if they would mind my storing some things there in the meantime. They told me that they had wanted to talk to me also,;"we want to ask your permission, to move out on the 24th of September already, on the public holiday, because we found a place.We need not wait for two months until the end of October." I replied softly: "it suits me very well." Lost for words I drove away from there... The love of the Father is so real; Haggai had spoken of the 24th of the ninth month and here the Lord intervened and changed their circumstances in such a way to suit us all, on the very day as predicted.(I realised this is a special Word for me,the Jewish calender not like ours!)

Truly, on the 24th we moved in! With the deepest Peace inside of me, I had moved within His Perfect Will. It was the solution to a lot of things; for special occasions such as birthdays we would eat and enjoy time together at my house.

13. IF THE LORD HIMSELF FIGHTS…

Haggai 2 verse 20 " The word of the Lord came to Haggai a second time on the twenty-fourth day of the month:
Verse 21"Tell Zerubbabel governor of Judah that I am going to shake the heavens and the earth.
Verse 22; I will overturn royal thrones and shatter the power of the foreign kingdoms. I will overthrow chariots and their drivers; horses and their riders will fall, each by the sword of his brother. Verse 23 "'On that day,' declares the Lord Almighty, 'I will take you, my servant Zerubbabel son of Shealtiel,' declares the Lord, 'and I will make you like my signet ring, for I have chosen you,' declares the Lord Almighty."

The kitchen cupboards underneath the sink was in decay and my heart was really aching. The cupboards would have to be replaced and I have just spent a lot of money on other changes to the house, so there wouldn't be money for the replacement of these cupboards as well. My husband been ashamed for our neighbours,witnessing the move. He took his daughter and her friend on a fishing trip , so I managed the move on my own. That Sunday evening during service, I could think of nothing other, the stinking kitchen cupboards and my mood,very heavy. Something told me to praise the Lord and hand it over. I started praising the Lord and focused on the service. That night, just before we fell asleep, my husband said: I asked the cabinet makers around the corner to come and have a look at that cupboard underneath the kitchen sink. I will have a new one installed for you." Oh, our Master! My husband,that very afternoon, still been agitated about the move.

A wonderful time in our life started developing here; just as it is mentioned in the Scriptures:"now I will build you up" We are living in a complex and two of my lady friends, lived there. Often, we walk over to each other's homes,having lovely prayer and social time together. I arranged my home to my liking, and I felt quite alive again. The liberation was sweet; it is just the same as work ethic- one should just get to a win-win situation for all parties involved. I went to visit a friend in the United Kingdom. As I was getting off the bus, she exclaimed: "what is different about you? You look so different... The weight that I had been noticing,on your face is no longer there!" I told her about moving back into my own home and it was amazing that she could see it on my face, immediately. The Lord alone can change our destiny. One evening my husband asked me in surprise, "why did you mention to me this morning that I should be wary of Linda (pseudonym)?" It stayed with me the whole of the next day... The words just flowed from my lips... I didn't know who this Linda was, but could it be Word from our Heavenly Father? My husband proceeded to tell me that he had run into her "accidentally" and that she had been a colleague of his, previously, while he had still been working. I noticed the Lord had made him aware of something, because he sounded rather upset or even uncomfortable about it. I could only pray: "Master, You know everything."

A while after that, the two of us went away for a weekend alone. That Friday evening ,he looked pale and very upset. He couldn't keep it to himself any longer and burst out. "Something terrible has happened. When Linda arrived at home last night, her husband, who was in a wheelchair, aimed his pistol at her when she walked into the house and shot her. She was killed instantly."

After that the cleaning girl, told me the full story. My husband and this Linda, had earlier, an affair and it had flared up once again, now while we were still married. This made me wonder if her husband had found out about it... Could it just as easily had been my husband who got shot and killed? I could see that he was broken. In silence we continued our journey. The Lord kept me calm. I had known there was still a very deeply disguised secret lurking... which I could clearly sense. We never spoke about this again. Jesus Christ Himself knows the what's and why's of our lives. But one thing I have learnt and that was that: that which I had to know, would always come into the Light. Even as a sinner, surely, my husband must have seen the Hand of God and heard His voice. I noticed him, starting to look up to this Jesus Christ whom I served, with much more respect. It wasn't just a passing phase, but a reality! To the very name, the Lord is able to call out third parties.The Father was warning him,stay away from that girl!

Mark 10 verse 9 NIV: "Therefore what God has joined together, let no one separate." Other versions say, "may no third party separate"! Not my words, but the Word of the Living God!!

One evening, my husband and one of his family members were sitting on our porch and looked at the church goers passing by. The family member made the most horrible comments about the people making their way to the Pentecostal church, where I also, on occasion visit . My heart was ripped into pieces by the shock of his words; that he could speak in such a crass way about the children of the Lord. At a previous occasion, he had much to say, to me,for visiting a church meeting, of a different nation.(In their area)

I had been so surprised about all these outbursts. That following Wednesday, this very family member called us very anxiously to share the bad news, he had lost his job. So, I have witnessed many acts of vengeance by God! I would never dare, to put up a fight with the Lord,s children.

I had seen how dangerous that can be. Years later, this man was saved by the Lord, he had converted. He died later of cancer, and every time he was hospitalised, he would call for me and we prayed together in love. There is nothing the Lord cannot do.

John 3 verse 16 "For God so loved the world that he gave his one and only Son, that whoever believes in him shall not perish but have eternal life." His eternal Life for all!!

14. THE DARKEST CLOUDS GATHER ABOVE...

Before we moved from my husband's house, there were a lot of serious altercations. The daughter complained of being caught in depression and her boyfriend told us she was unhappy at home and that she had had a lot of complaints which mostly would of course been about me; but I sensed, something wasn't right. I know only one road, that be the one of prayer and again, prayer... Many days I would go and lie down on her bed and called upon the Lord to break these evil forces. I had even secretly anointed her pillows. This did achieve a measure of peace for a while. Sister Hope told me a story: "You know, Sister, there had been times before my husband converted that I had been so deeply desperate and then the Master taught me something important. I studied,
 Esther 4 verse 3 "In every province to which the edict and order of the king came, there was great mourning among the Jews, with fasting, weeping and wailing. Many lay in sackcloth and ashes."
I took that text to heart and actually applied it. When the solution to a problem kept escaping me, I would fast and throw a sack onto the floor, spread ashes onto it and wearing old clothes, I would pray on top of that sack, sometimes even rolling in the ashes. All this, in secret, when there would be nobody else around. I have seen the Lord break the powers of satan when I called unto Him so desperately for a solution."

It is only for us who are truly and desperately seeking solutions; as the Scriptures call it "to cry out in mourning". It is a horrible experience to go through, finding your child involved with drugs, and related things. You can get physical ill, of the shock, if the Lord doesn't help you.

I have applied this many times and still do, to this day. Many times, I have joined fellow worshippers who had been in harsh battles in prayer on sack and ashes. We even prayed like this for our own weaknesses which had a tight hold on us.

Just like Sister Hope did, I found that, especially in the case of whitch doctor spells, Jesus would always come up with solutions, particularly after prayer sessions like these. I believe, as many other people also say, "accept the methods which work for you and let go of the rest". If it is not for you, so be it, but I have received, many wonderful resolutions in this manner.

There had been phone calls from parents, of the daughter's friends, telling us that they had seen her very drunk in public places. Her father refused to believe any of this. She would then call these parents, while he listened: "what nonsense are you spreading about me!?" And that would satisfy him.

The episode about the weed that previous time was still lingering between us. I kept on praying: "Master, please bring the truth into the light."

One Sunday afternoon, a few of her girlfriends' parents stopped outside our house. I knew immediately that something big was amiss. She had once again been out for the weekend. My husband went outside to meet the people there, as he didn't want to invite them inside. I looked through the window as they spoke with him; I watched as he went down onto his heels and sat down on the grass. He couldn't stand upright. I heard them telling ,that all their children as well as his daughter had been caught using prohibited substances. She phoned a little later and told him "Daddy, all will be fine, I am already in a place to get the help I need." He yelled at me:" There, the wheel has turned, are you happy now?" That was the only way he could handle it. He had to fight with someone, while he was forgetting how I begged him that we should rather pick her up at night when she was out. Her friends' parents had taken turns to do it, because then,you are able to see first-hand in what state the child is… He never deemed it necessary. All along it had been the drugs that had made her so depressed. It plays havoc with the emotions and causes severe ups and downs.

Well, in the end, it wasn't so easy. Thousands of Rands later and severe arguments, she wasn't able to get free from the drugs. The only way was through Jesus Christ. But this girl and her father kept on rejecting Him. "We will show everybody we will beat this."

A lot of things disappeared from the house as well as his favourite old guitar. I don't even want to write about this, but so many parents, have to go through this. One evening he was about to take a shower and put his wallet on the windowsill. A hand came through the open window... He was broken: his beloved daughter was a thief! At one point he told me, he considered her death, to have been easier for him. A long-time school friend of hers had just returned from a Rehabilitation Centre and came to visit her. That night they got hold of drugs and injected themselves. She then came home. His parents had been away for the weekend. The next say, their cleaning girl, found his corpse in the house. Apparently, because he had been clean for a while, he had overdosed and stopped breathing. There is no bigger hell than the one of drugs.

I was confronted about this, by her friends mothers,they felt she causes it, but at the end of the day, it was the boy's choice to use it, wasn't it? The daughter was in a terrible state,we once more tried to get her the help she needed. Sister Hope and I came together and prayed and trusted. At this point, he was also crying out for help, so much so that he had driven out to Sister Hope with me, with a gift of fried fish, which he had caught himself. He appreciated the prayers a lot.

The daughter had once again released herself from the Karl Bremer Centre, after the first withdrawal phase. They give a patient only one chance. The counsellors as well as the mother of the deceased friend came to beg my husband to obtain a court order to get her into rehab. He refused... There are parents who act with strength and conviction, but there are others who allow themselves to be dragged along... He could not get to the point of "tough love". Only the Master can help with that. I had met other parents who were faithful to the Lord and they had begged Him to harden their own hearts. One day, before these events, we ran into an old friend of my husbands at the sports club. During our conversation he told us about his brother who had become addicted to drugs. He had robbed his family bare for drug money. His mother kept protecting him and felt sorry for him. One day he demanded money from his mom and began pushing and shoving her. She then realised it had gone too far and got a court order for him to get treatment.

While he was away, he phoned his mother. When she heard his voice, she immediately said, "I don't have a son" and then put the phone down. His brother told us, that shocked him so much, that he is to this day, seven years later, clean of drugs.

I have personally met with dear ones in the Lord, who had come clean of drugs through Jesus Christ and who had done great spiritual work with me. One young brother told me: after he had accepted Jesus Christ into his life, and after hearing many nights how his grandmother was praying for him, he had fasted for a few days and he was saved, without any withdrawal symptoms. There is definitely supernatural healing at work as well!

The way I see it, is that there is only salvation in Christ. I know of a psychologist who in his work with addicts, would ask them if they are prepared to accept Jesus into their lives; if they don't, he replies that he doesn't have another way to treat them.

He had to sell his house to cover all the cost. He bought a small flat, for her.

One night my husband came in late from the sports club and subsequently fell asleep very quickly from too much to drink. Something made me to have a look at his wallet. I found numerous banking slips, where he had been withdrawing money... I had such a fright. Most of the money from the sale of the house had been gone. I saw with my own eyes that he had been withdrawing between twenty and thirty thousand Rand a month. I realised he was buying the drugs for her, so that she wouldn't steal. She had been jailed numerous times for petty crimes to pay for drugs. She told me once how a person would be falling all over the back of a police van, because there is no place to get a grip and hold on. I laugh along, at hearing things like this, but know, this road I was on, I had not ever even heard of before.

I fell onto my knees on the floor, and the darkness of hopelessness came over me. While I was talking to my Master, I was trembling, and my mind raced in circles; what will happen when the money runs out? Which seemed very close in the near future... "Master, help, what will become of me? They are going to force me to help! I cannot use Your money for drugs!"

I didn't get any answers and I became even more panicked while he was sleeping. Suddenly, a thought, as gentle as a light breeze, entered my mind: "If you do not start praising Me right now and so come back into the faith, you will fall into a deep pit of depression and stay there." I was scared. This was the master's Voice. Still feeling as hopeless, I started chanting:" I PRAISE YOU MASTER, I PRAISE YOU MASTER, YOU ARE MY SHEPHERD!"

The next day, if panic would start to, well up in me, I repeated: "I PRAISE YOU MASTER!" I kept at this for days. The money did run out and It was a hard time. Sometimes, he didn't even have money for cigarettes and the Lord doesn't allow me to just give. Then he would do chores, such as mowing the lawn, for which I would pay him. Sometimes I would give him things, such as a music player which he had given me before. I knew he would sell that, to give his daughter money for drugs.

The Master chastised me for this spirit of "feeling sorry" because I was aiding something wrongful. I learnt how dangerous it is to feel sorry in the wrong way, not the way the Lord wants. My own money started running through my fingers, like water. I had still been contributing a tenth of my income to the Lord, but things started seriously going wrong. One day, as I was praying and asking the Lord's advice about what had happened, an answer came to me in the evening breeze. "I did not advise you to hand out everything for this sort of situation; the only way for Me to teach you, that you can be helped, is if you also lost, money!" I had a fright because I never thought it wrong of me to help. "Oh, dear Lord, forgive me, save me, restore me from sin." This is my personal experience; there is such a thing as giving in a wrongful way. You are giving away that which the Lord has blessed you with! To this day, I have not been able to buy another music player and I do miss it dearly to be able to listen to gospel music on the christian radio station. At the moment I only have a cheap radio which has disturbances and moves out of tuning very quickly. But it is because I have given away my blessings to Cash Crusaders.

My husband received monthly pension from his deceased wife, but it was too little to cover his monthly expenses. I was not aware of the amount,that he received, our bank accounts were separated. In these dark times, I noticed that even some of our meat was disappearing. I summoned that it must have been taken for the daughter... While I was climbing this steep uphill, sometimes I could only crawl, I suddenly received relief.

Only people who have been in this situation, would know the toll so much stress has on one's physical body.

One night, I saw the white powder in his wallet, and I realised he had begun buying from the dealers, for her, so that she wouldn't be at risk of being arrested again. As if it would be OK for him to be arrested instead! The situation was very dire, because I did not agree with what he was doing. I had to tell everything to the Lord Jesus Christ, on my knees in secret, in silence. While I was so very tired from all the tension at home, I noticed an advertisement. Our work having a project in England, over a period of six weeks. I immediately applied for it and prayed about it, together with my prayer buddies. Everything pointed to the fact that it would be His will for me to go. In that time, My husband also felt it would be good for me to go, because he would be able to devote all his time to his children, because the son now suffered from a broken relationship.

Oh, the Lord... I was the first one, from our hospital, to be chosen for the project!

1 Corinthians 10 verse 13: "No temptation has overtaken you except what is common to mankind. And God is faithful; he will not let you be tempted beyond what you can bear. But when you are tempted, he will also provide a way out so that you can endure it."

What a loving Father had control of my life? It was a wonderful experience; on my days off, I travelled just where I wanted, with my food allowance money. As I mentioned earlier, I also visited Scotland, I came home inspired and with renewed courage and a lot of mountains in the sea.

The financial situation was still very poor. I noticed an advertisement of a sports club looking for a manager. I showed it to my husband and helped him to apply for it. There were twenty-five applications. When the lady called me to advise that my husband had got the job, both of us cried!It changed our situation so much for the better. I had much less stress and the additional income had been just enough.

Our dear Saviour is near, our Loving Saviour... I sang the well-known hymn. Now I had learnt what faith was; even though you don't feel or see anything, just keep saying out loud "Praise the Lord"... with the slightest spark of hope, He can do the impossible for us.

Proverbs 3 verse 6: "Trust in the Lord with all your heart and lean not on your own understanding; in all your ways submit to him, and he will make your paths straight."

Mark 10 verse 27 "Jesus looked at them and said, "With man this is impossible, but not with God; all things are possible with God."

Yes, I surely would have fallen into that dark well, had I not learnt from the Holy Spirit that just a faint whisper "I believe, Lord" could bring His Hand into action.

Hebrew 11 verse 6: "And without faith it is impossible to please God, because anyone who comes to him must believe that he exists and that he rewards those who earnestly seek him."

Anyone who wants to come to him must believe that God exists and that he rewards those who sincerely seek Him."

15. SUMMARY OF THE SITUATION

After I had seen the white powder in his wallet, I told him about it. It was supposedly someone from the club's and he had to take it away... or something like that... Almost as if he had been very ashamed, that I had seen it.He came less and less. He would sleep over at friends or at his daughter's. I didn't ask what was going on. With Jesus on your side, you have great Peace. As I had placed him above the Lord, in the past,now, I must place Jesus first.

Everything became easier for me. I wasn't carrying the full weight of the situation on my shoulders. I had to protect myself,it was like a whirlpool pulling downwards into the darkness. For him, things became much worse. I was desperate for his sake and I could see his stress. While I was pleading with the Lord, I read the story of Noah and the ark.

Genesis 6 verse 16;"You shall make a window for the ark,and finish it to a cubid from the top;and set the door of the ark in the side of it,...

"Genesis 7 verse 16;"And those that entered ...entered as God has commanded him,AND THE LORD CLOSED IT BEHIND HIM.'

It became clear to me... There had been only one look-out point from the ark and that was upwards. This meant that Noah could not look out to the sides and see people drowning. The Lord , closed the door from the outside.

So, the Lord, was busy with my husband, and I was the one in the ark, He had closed the door from the outside for me. I am not able to handle it, if I was to witness, what he was going through; all for the redemption of his soul.

On one occasion he came to fetch me to go out for a meal together. It was our wedding anniversary. My diary script for the day had been about peace in the eye of the storm. I read it to him and told him that if we confess our sins, He, the Lord, would change our affairs drastically. He looked panicked and said he couldn't confess his sins before me, but he did however kneel down beside me. That day, I prayed as never before; I poured out my whole heart. I told the Lord that I had never wanted this kind of marriage that we had; I had wanted it to be like that of my parents.

I asked the Lord of hosts, to forgive him; that he had not been brought up in a God -fearing house and therefore did not know how to live in the Lord. I asked for forgiveness for every time that I myself had done wrong to his children and to him. I cannot repeat everything here, but I really poured my heart out before Abba Father.

The might of the Lord came down to us; when I opened my eyes, I saw that tears were running from his eyes. He said: "oh my wife, you have taken me far away, now". He tried to give me a hug, but his arms were heavy. The Power of the Living God was upon him. I asked him; "What is holding you back, from accepting the Lord?" He replied: "I wish I knew, but it is not what you think." (I think he meant other women.) I went on: "Today I am asking your forgiveness for everything I had done badly to your family or caused your family to stumble or where I have hurt you and I also forgive you unconditionally for where you had done wrong to me. If anything should happen after today; should one of us die; or should you want to divorce me or drift away from me, I set you free, I am also free before the Lord.

All of this happened on our wedding anniversary.

We never went out for dinner that evening. I was in seventh heaven of happiness, as though he would give his life to Jesus the very next day. I was in a bubble… drifting on high air… nothing else mattered. While I am driving, my radio is tuned in to Radio Tygerberg. There was a testimony from a retired evangelist who had gone back to England, to his home, there. While the boat entered the harbour, he heard an orchestra playing and people gathered round. "Yes" he thought to himself, "I have worked very hard for the Lord and I deserve this reception." As he walked out, it was all, for a soccer team and not for him. Deeply disappointed he thought to himself, that he had also done great things. He,then heard a soft voice within, "Son, you are not home yet; there, trumpets will blow for you." At that moment my bubble burst, as I realised then, that I was not yet home with this issue.

Truthfully, after that, my husband came home even less. What a wonderful God we are serving. He does things, only the right way. We had to exchange forgiveness. It was as though the Father , been steering the separation in His own way.

At that point I was living (he, once every three weeks, or so, for one night at a time, there) in a big house with a big garden. I noticed a beautiful little house in a retirement village. My heart was on it! I was just over fifty, fifty beautiful years, young... He had a huge fright when I told him about it. The Lord's help was everywhere, out of the blue I received a cash offer on my own property, and I moved to the retirement village. My brothers and sisters in the Faith helped with the move. It was like, when Abraham packed up his belongings and moved away. It was a much smaller place, but everything fit in snuggly, even my piano found a place. A few beds and mattresses hung from the garage ceiling and the bicycle was mounted on the wall, but everything was done very neatly. When everything was in, we prayed together and the brothers in the Lord, anointed the house with oil and prayed that only those whom Jesus would want inside, would enter here. Another sister in the Lord, helped me to unpack and make everything tidy. Now I have a wonderful spiritual family around me.

My husband said he would like to come and see the new place. We made an appointment for the next day. I heard nothing from him, by 12 o' clock, I thought he wasn't coming at all and that I was waiting in vain. I drove out to Sister Hope's and prayed there. On my way there, I found him next to the road, taking a stroll to his daughter's place for exercise. He never asked to come over again and he never showed up there. That prayer we had together on the night of our anniversary, had been our farewell, and it came from the Lord.

Sometimes we would see each other when he would come to pick up something from the hospital. We chatted nicely and have peace between us. I have heard, that at this point, his circumstances, been much worse. He had lost his vehicle as well. His daughter now had a 5-year old son, whom he loved very much. During one of our chats at the hospital, he burst out in tears and told me that the little boy had been taken away from the mother and placed with the father, she neglected the child, He wasn't allowed to see the boy either. I asked him whether my prayer group and youth members, who had been freed from drug abuse, by Jesus Christ, could come over to pray for her and he replied "does she want to be helped?". This frightened me, because I sensed from this reply, that his hope is gone, for her to recover.

He is walking, where he wanted to go, lived with friends close to his work. He was known, as a wealthty man.The drugs have used all his money.His friends, friends of his deceased wife, supported him well with his daughter, his son and his grandson.

One night I dreamt that he had cried so much, his nose was red. In the dream, I told him that, if he confesses right now before the Lord, that he was guilty for his daughter's fall into disgrace, because he never wanted to listen to advice and intervene to change her behaviour, that the Lord would change the situation and things wil turn for the better for him.

In the dream she wants to fight me, wants nothing to do with prayer. But, in the dream, he however did confess that he was guilty.

A few days later, I saw him, where he was working. I explained to him that the Lord sometimes spoke to people through dreams and delivered messages that way. I told him about my dream and said that if he prayed like that day,at our anniversary. If he would confess his sins to the Lord, the Lord certainly will change his life. He is a very proud man; he just clung to his cigarette and started shaking,and crying uncontrollably. He turned around and walked away, afraid that his friends would see him crying. I called after him: "Remember, Jesus loves you very much!" I was on my way to one of our services. I was shivering and it felt as if my whole being was shaking; I have never seen him like that. I felt almost hysterical. I wanted to help, but I didn't know how. The thought of the ark entered my mind again, with the window, up above. At the service, I asked a trusted sister to pray together. The next day, she called me up. She said that while she was praying, she could feel that I was on the brink of hysteria. I was in that state for days on end. I just couldn't see any solution to how I could help him.A very dear,older sister in the Lord,phoned me,from Worcester.

I told her what had happened and what,I felt. Magnificently she explained the situation; she said the Lord, was giving her a picture: "Sister, I can clearly see,it is about his daughter he is crying; it is not about you. Sister has to stay aware,away and sober about this.You cannot carry his weight,you are not the Lord.Let the Lord do His work,get out of the way!"

"Thank you, Master" and once again, I was shocked back into sobriety.

A year later I saw him and truly, he must have gone and prayed on his own, confessing to the Lord that he was guilty in his daughter's demise, because he looked much better, even a little happier. I told him "Oh, I am grateful to see that things are looking much better for you" and I drove away. I really felt relieved that things looked better for him. "You in your corner, and I in mine" a little chorus repeated in my mind. In our conversation he told me about his new car and that he was still living with his friends. His daughter came over every day for food or something. His grandson came to visit him every other weekend. "Do you know, he is such a normal, lovely child, after all that he had gone through with his mother...". Oh... the love of the Father...

Mathew 5 verse 44... "But now I tell you; love your enemies and pray for those who persecute you, so that you may become the sons of your Father.

FOR HE MAKES HIS SUN TO SHINE ON BAD AND GOOD PEOPLE ALIKE AND GIVES RAIN TO THOSE WHO DO GOOD AND TO THOSE WHO DO EVIL" ...

John 3 verse 19 "And this is the condemnation, that Light is come into this world, and men LOVED DARKNESS RATHER THAN LIGHT, BECAUSE THEIR DEEDS WERE EVIL" ...

16. TRAVELS WITH SISTER HOPE

After a few months of praying together and every so often attending her services, she mentioned that they were going to a small country town, about a nine-hour journey from the Cape.

At that time, I had had a small operation and I still had two weeks sick leave. I offered to take them and then, rest there. Their pastor, a real shepherd, he sent an elder along with us, because he felt,we as women should not take on this journey. The elder is also a good driver, we could take turns driving. They paid for all the fuel and also provided money for food along the road, true family ministry. I booked lodging at a game farm ,just outside of the town,they stayed with church members.

Here my wonderful,learning career of Christ like living commenced. Our journey had been very blessed. We prayed a lot the nine-hour journey. They pray at every stopping point and thank the Lord for His protection up to that point. When we start moving again, they pray once again for protection for the journey still ahead.

For the first time in my life I heard the prayer: "Lord, help us not to get angry with one another along the way, but endure each other in peace." They explained to me they always pray this according to what Joseph said to his brothers.

Genesis 45 verse 24 "Then he sent his brothers away, and as they were leaving, he said to them, "Don't quarrel on the way." The New American Standard Bible describes it this way: "So he sent his brothers away, and as they departed, he said to them. "Do not quarrel on the journey" with reference for quarrel "agitated".

Well, what does it matter, I thought? But as time passed, I began to understand; the Holy Spirit works only within unity. I asked the Master to give me His spirit. I had an intense desire to receive and experience the Spirit of Jesus Christ. I cannot create it for myself. I would decide that I will not become irritable, the very next "Sister, can we pull over, I have a need" I would be tested… Then I would just smile, but inside, I would be very irritated… "we could have been so much further on the road already"... If we pray, when we start driving again, I find myself not to be within that full freedom and happiness. Then I would shoot up a silent prayer: "Master, forgive me my lovelessness and impatience, restore me in Your Likeness," then complete peace and joy would once again overcome me. The road of laying down the self becomes a wonderful journey because as you grow in it, little things do not matter to you so much and His Peace stays within you. I found that I just have to keep asking for it in prayer. Sometimes I failed the exam, but my Father stays true; He always gives me another opportunity to write the exam again.

James 5 verse 9: "Don't grumble against one another, brothers and sisters, or you will be judged. The Judge is standing at the door!"

I once saw the following quotation on the internet: 'Arguments drag out because one is too stubborn to forgive and the other is too proud to apologise!While we,passing, Moorreesburg, the one sister mentioned: "Sister, while we were praying, I saw in my mind's eye those anchors which they throw down in a storm to keep the boat stable. Sister is in a storm now, and while you are out with us, to do the Lord's work, He is going to give you the weight for your anchor, so that your boat will not topple over."

Later it was proven over and over again that this was indeed the Wisdom of my Father. Huge storms had broken around me, while I was still there, but thank you Master, my Anchor had held me stable.

I slept well in the little cottage on the game farm. Sister Hope called me early in the morning to check in on me. She said, "oh, it feels as if you are so far away from us". Later years, we would laugh over this, us two. Her daughters said, "Mommy, this sister is just like the one in Fiela's child (a book written by Daleen Mathee,about a coloured mother raising a white baby,found next to the road,her love for this child) Many people who knew us called me "Fiela'child". The love of Christ is stronger than any race or colour or address!!!

The cleaner came in and while I was talking to her about Jesus, she told me she was a child of Jesus.She had dreamt that people would come from Cape Town and they would support her in prayer. I quickly called Sister Hope and told them about this. They were free and I immediately went to fetch them. when the cleaner saw the team, she shouted out loud, "thank you JESUS, it is just how they looked in my dream!" The Holy Spirit came down and the team rejoiced just as loud and thanked the Lord, while the tears flowed freely. I have never witnessed anything as wondrous as this. They didn't know each other but they hugged each other and praised our wonderful Lord. I felt a tightening from within and I couldn't understand why I was not feeling so excited. Suddenly there was a knock on the door. I never noticed the Rondawel was separated into two parts, only a thin wall, that there had been people on the other side.

They had quickly called the owner about the noise. The caretaker stood there; her eyes wide with fright. In the background you could hear "thank you Lord… thank you Lord…" "There is a complaint about noise, from here". Then she saw the cleaner! "What are you doing here? Go back to work!". "Madam, it is my lunch break", she said. I am ashamed. Sister Hope, and the other sister,was very slow, I,was in a hurry to get to the cleaner.Our Father, knew,meeting to be within her lunch break, otherwise she would have lost her job. There I realised once again, I still had a long way to go, to become more like the Master. "We do apologise, we didn't realise, other people around." The neighbours glared at us; we must have looked rather strange to them.

We took the cleaner's address and she continued with her work. The pastor,of that branch,organised alternative lodging for me at a guest house in town. Now we still had to get past the management of the game farm, because I had booked for a whole week. They actually looked very relieved that I wanted to leave, they had me pay only for the one night that I had stayed there!

It is our custom to be considerate towards others. We weren't vigilant and careful, like the Scripture has it "not in self-control."All worked , for the better, I became even closer to the dear ones.

I found the guest house owner and his family also somewhat suspicious and unfriendly, probably because I was working with people which are from a different nation. The lesson I learn from this; not to pay too much attention to the actions of others. As Sister Hope put it: "People don't have heaven for you; we are going to the heaven of Jesus Christ, and the way there, is described in the bible,not their heaven!" At this point in time, I was still very much alive within my own self. Sister Hope and the others stayed in a large house but due to circumstances there, some windows were broken, and the wind was very cold at night. I gave them my warm gown and a warm jacket to sleep under. She was already in her sixties and her knees would ache, when it was cold. In the mornings she would be so filled with joy and she would minister to that family ,with the love and support of Jesus Christ. She never lodged a complaint with the church about the circumstances she had to endure. She was living self-denying to the full extent and I could see the power of His Resurrection in her life. We were asked to visit an older sister. Her circumstances had been dire. Her son been released from jail and his wife was living an aggressive life. She was treating the old lady badly. Even her own daughter would drop in and give her a hard time. The pastor-mother accompanied us. She reprimanded them and spoke to them in harsh words. I noticed that they were not taking in any of what the Pastor's wife is saying to them. It was as though a wall, been erected between them. Suddenly it came to me, that I should wash their feet and as I wash them, I should cut off the evil spirits which were now in them,all in Jesus's name. Softly, I whispered it, to Sister Hope, because I had to stay within the order of the Word... I cannot take my own lead here. She nodded her head and I asked for a bowl of water and a washcloth. With a childlike spirit, I asked the man, "may I wash your feet?" He had a big fright, he was still very big within himself, but he agreed. I knelt before him, he took off his shoes; the Master's Love came down unto me and it was no longer myself, but the Only Father, who loves the world, which is being lost; I wash and I pray softly: "Jesus, you alone ; You break these bonds". The next moment, he burst into tears and asked the Lord to save him. While Sister Hope and the team prayed for him, I started washing the woman's feet as well and I said the same prayer. She also burst into tears and called for Jesus. Lastly, I took her own daughter, who seemed very hard and had a real fighting spirit. She too broke before the might of the Lord. In tears, all three of them asked their elderly mother for forgiveness. It was so beautiful to have all three of them that Wednesday evening at the prayer meeting. He had put on a suit and even his complexion was different. It looked to me as if he shone from within. His wife looked beautiful in her church attire. His daughter also looked pretty. They stayed on the Lord's road, but I heard he died just a few years later.

A few years ago, out of the blue, I received a WhatsApp message, and I didn't know who it was from. Then Sister Hope explained to me that it was from them; her husband had died but she was still within Jesus's ways. For months I received daily beautiful messages from her.

Something in me came alive that day; even to give just one small cup of water to a child of the Lord, brings the greatest joy to your inner being.

The next day we visited a young couple who had lost a baby. They lived in a humble zinc-shack, as we neared the little house, a great thankfulness came over me; it was a privilege that they would allow me, someone from a different race, into their home. All of this, due to Sister Hope. It was a one-room dwelling and everything was very tidy. The young brother was filled with faith and told us how he prayed "Father I want to ask you today for chicken, pumpkin and potatoes.There is no food in the house and I don't have money, but You have everything and I am your son and I really want to have a nice plate of food for my whole family." He went on and told us, that day he was riding with his bicycle to town and nothing happened, it was after 1pm. He greeted another sister from church, and she called to him, "brother, I feel that I must give you some of my chicken". Now he just needed the rest and he went along. Later that afternoon someone said they wanted to put a parcel onto the bicycle's carrier, to drop off at his house. When he delivered it, he gave him R15 (2008).With that he quickly went to buy vegetables and that night they were eating exactly what he had asked his Father.

This kind of testimony also encouraged me. There is nothing which our Father cannot do for us. After the prayer team encouraged them, Sister Hope asked him: "Brother, what can we ask on your behalf this morning from Jesus... what is on your heart?" The wind had been blowing and was very cold through holes in the walls of the shack, I was expecting that he would ask for a few new sheets of corrugated iron or for a new house. He replied: "Sister, I really want to understand my dreams; when is it from the Father and also what they mean. I will also be very grateful if we could have another child and if it can be another girl. I am grateful for the little boy I have." I sat astounded and all that entered my mind was "seek first the Kingdom of God and all else will be added to you."

A few years later I got a phone call from Sister Hope "Sister come over quickly, I have a big surprise". Well I arrived there, there was this brother with his wife and their new baby girl. I told them that day, that when their baby girl arrived, they should give her my second name. They did that, and here I was, sitting with her in my arms. The Master had uplifted him with such a good job, he could buy a good name, bakkie. It could only be Jesus Christ who had done it.

So, the days flew by and we visited many people and prayed together. Sister Hope felt the guest house was so expensive, they should rather organise accommodation for me. Very nervously one sister offered a bedroom in her house. Her husband was also very nervous about it; there had never been a white person in their house before, let alone sleep over there! Sister Hope brought them into the Light; "Sister is a child of Jesus… as the Word mentions.

Romans 12 verse 5; "so in Christ we, though many, form one body, and each member belongs to all the others"

1 Peter 2 verse 9; "But you are a chosen people, a royal priesthood, a Holy nation, God's special possession, that you may declare the praises of Him who called you out of darkness into His wonderful light."

American standard version: "BUT YOU ARE A CHOSEN RACE, A ROYAL PRIESTHOOD…"

Revelation 27: "Whoever has ears, let them hear what the Spirit says to the churches. To the one who is victorious, I will give the right to eat from the tree of life, which is in the paradise of God."

To the one who conquers,I will grant to eat of the tree of life, which is in the paradise of God.

I took a lesson from that part of my life… all races on both sides are within Christ the "chosen race". Something brand new in Christ!! It is something which I have to conquer and outlive; that "you look different than I" in every aspect of my life. I thank the Lord that he found me good enough to put through these challenges. We close that door", I am different"specially in south Africa!". truly, that was a huge test for me. I have to admit, I was a little uncomfortable. They had just built on a new room where everything had not yet been completed. There was new bedding on the bed, new towels, new facecloth. While I was pulling, into the yard, I realised how far I was yet from "we are one". The people of the house were really uncomfortable; everyone was too afraid to speak; we ate in silence. I didn't sleep much that night… their uneasiness was tangible. If Jesus Christ doesn't free you from something, you will not be free from it. On both sides of our different races, we have high walls of separation.

There, I realised that I have to trust the Master for greater salvation. Many days I still wanted to be the white sister instead of just a sister, in the Lord. As time went on, the Lord worked within me and brought it into full completion. Later on, the Scriptures opened for me:

1 Chronicles 11 verse 1 All Israel joined David at Hebron and said."Look, we are your flesh and blood!

My heart, must become one with them, and we really came into unity. The Lord Jesus Christ did just that great work, until today. They are flesh of my flesh or I am flesh of theirs. That was the first step to setting me free from preconceived ideas.

Before, we left that town back to Cape Town, I learned something wonderful. The elder who was traveling with us, came to each of us. "Sister, forgive me if I have caused you to stumble or maybe made you feel bad, we must go in peace onto the Road, anything can happen." Baffled, I managed to say, "I forgive Elder, where I have stumbled and forgive me also for where I have caused the elder to stumble." I was very happy to forgive and to get forgiveness, because to be together for a week, is not always easy!

Yes, reader, I had been in the Baptist Bible School for a period of time, I know the Pentecostal churches of the Cape very well… I have friends everywhere. Never had I experienced what I had experienced on this trip. The true Godliness as it is written in the Bible. The Master also unlocked wisdom for me. They are truly "Royal Priesthood". So, we all openly asked for and gave each other forgiveness before we took to the road again. Godly peace was on us all.

Acts 2 verse 1 "when the day of Pentecost had come, they were all together in one place,

Verse 2 "AND SUDDENLY A SOUND CAME FROM HEAVEN LIKE A RUSHING VIOLENT WIND, AND IT FILLED THE WHOLE HOUSE WHERE THEY WERE SITTING.

When we were leaving town, we all bought some lamb, and we

received a lot of other things as gifts. The car was very full. I was worried deep in my heart; I was only driving an ordinary Toyota and to me it seemed that we had overloaded the car. I just prayed in silence. All of a sudden, Sister Hope started praying out loud "Father, I thank you for Sister's new car, thank you for the angels whom You are sending to lift the car and carry us to Cape Town. Master, you are aware, how full the car is right now." I had such a fright!

Yes, even my thoughts the Master opened up to them. With the biggest joy I have ever known, we drove away from there; singing: "There is Pentecostal in heaven! That is true, there is Pentecostal in heaven, that is true".

Acts 2 verse 4 "All of them were filled with the Holy Spirit and began to speak in other tongues as the Spirit enabled them."

I truly experienced it in that car, we were in unity of spirit, the power and joy as it is in Heaven; we experienced something of that. Everything of the cold and the hardship here and there, now was far gone. Jesus Christ through the Holy Spirit was with us in the car.

I never thought it possible; that new car Sister Hope had mentioned in her prayer... A few months later I received a special bonus and I bought myself a brand-new Citroën. I saw this; when I do something for my neighbour in all humility, the Lord opens the showers of heaven for me.

This is how the traveling in my leave-time began. My husband loved fishing, so when he would go away fishing with his friends, I went fishing, for Jesus. It was a learning school for me at the feet of an anointed of the Lord.

We went to Walvis Bay a few times. First, we went by bus and later we took the plane, for the sake of Sister Hope's health. When we would leave there, the dear ones would cry and hug us. There I saw true love in Jesus Christ. I took her everywhere where her congregation had people. What an honour and privilege.

On occasion we were close to Plettenberg Bay in a holiday resort. Early, that morning, Sister Hope called me. I was awake; she asked me to wake the other sister who had accompanied us so that we could pray. The sister however wanted to rest some more. "Sister, we are going to rest in heaven, here, we have to fight, the devil, he never gets tired; we cannot always act according to what our bodies feel, He will give us strength , we shall rest at His time. Now sister must get up, He is calling on us." That morning, deep and dark plans of the enemy were revealed to us and we could cut it off in Jesus's Name. We had to get up,for that work, later in the afternoon we went to rest. We visited that congregation, and the pastor has never met me before. He looked at me, looked at me again and then he asked Sister Hope, "Mother, did you bring us a white Sister today?" She replied "No Pastor, she is just a child of the Lord,". She had a boldness in the Lord when she had to speak the truth.

At one of our ministries the chief elder confessed, at first it had been difficult for him and his family to become used to me,in their midst. He had been jailed in the struggle against "the apartheid". Although he became very wealthy post-apartheid, his children never knew apartheid, they too had trouble accepting me at first, because of what their father had told them, what he has been put through,Jesus Christ took all that away and many a time,we were laughing and joking together.We really became one in Jesus,but it is always good to talk it over,to get healed.

We talked about the Scripture again and also about forgiveness and unity in the Spirit etc.

It was for many of them also a test of their faith, accepting ,me in their midst. Many of the loved ones were openly suspicious towards me. Didn't I have a church in my area? Why was I joining them? I gave them my testimony. About the Lord tasking me with the Word as I mentioned before, "and you have to unite your heart with them fully". In all honesty, there were times that I didn't understand. I was the only one of my nation in the ministry. But when I see how they are living according to the Word, and how they do not back off at any evil power, because they are so finely and well trained by the Master Himself in His Might only, then I understand.

1 Kings 10 verse 4 "When the queen of Sheba saw all the wisdom of Solomon and the palace he had built

Verse 5 the food on his table, the seating of his officials, the attending servants in their robes, his cupbearers, and the burnt offerings he made at[a] the temple of the Lord, she was overwhelmed."

Sister Hope had just like king Solomon gotten her wisdom from the Lord

Himself, for every aspect of her life. Her actions, her sitting or standing. It was very important how you conducted yourself with the Holy Spirit in your midst.

Once, we were ministering to a brother and I was sitting on a chair, with him on the floor in front of me. I was wearing a skirt which reached beneath my knees, but I sat with my legs crossed. She called me outside and asked me in the greatest love, "would Sister please in the name of holiness, rather sit with your knees straight because the skirt is moving up and it can be a stumbling block, for the brother, surely my sister understands?" The Spirit of the Lord was so tangible there, I had been so grateful for the help from her.

Last night I was watching something on a Christian channel, and I noticed the sister sitting there with her legs crossed and her thighs bare on the screen… I felt grateful all over again; how many times before that, had I not also sat in such a wrong position. Thank you, Lord, for the salvation. "Help me Father, let Your Kingdom come through me, in Heaven, also here on earth. Master, I seek to have Your wisdom, like Solomon and like You, when You were on the earth. Yes Lord, I want to obey you like You obeyed Your Father impossible for a human, but possible through You."

17. THE SUN SET FOR SISTER HOPE…

Yes, Sister Hope got older. Our unity in Christ grew over a period of twenty years into a tightly bound unit. Her wish was that I should write a book about how we, from two different nations became one person in Christ. About the great work which Christ can do across the divisions of nations. I had wanted to name the book "When brown and white become as white as snow in Him"… but the "less perfect" stands out way higher for me.

I found myself in Plettenberg Bay, at the most beautiful residence by the sea. Irealised,that Sister Hope's time on earth was drawing to an end. I became anxious and my chest felt congested. Us and a younger sister who had now been living with Sister Hope, was doing everything together. This was the first time in many years that I had broken away without them.

Sundays after service we would eat together, then we would pray together, rest a while before the evening service. I would just stay there and lie behind her or the other sister's back. We became like one family unit. On Friday evenings we prayed together, on every off-day I would be at Sister Hope's. One day I decided to take a drive out to the sea, without Sister Hope. But my inner soul was restless. I stopped and asked the Master what was wrong?

Matthew 26 verse 11. "You will always have the poor people with you, but you will not always have me. What she did was to pour this perfume on my body to get me ready for burial."

I realised I had to spend every available minute with Sister Hope, because I wasn't going to have her around forever. I was so happy for buying time with her! Every minute that I had not been at work, I was with her. Many times, we busy with the work of the Lord. Today, I carry her wisdom and everything that she had learnt from the Master, within me. Today, I am working the Lord's acre and I know why I had to be with her all the time; because I had to learn everything I could from her.

Now I was sitting in Plettenberg Bay and I didn't know how I was going to carry on living without her on this earth.

While I sat there, so anxious, two little sparrows flew right in through the window and sat down on the carpet. I was in such a deep turmoil about the future, that I sat motionless. After a while, they flew out again. And then I found my answer from the Father of the Universe: "My child, just as I am taking care of the sparrows, I will look after you." The Lord's Peace came over me; all the anxiety left me, and I had courage for my future. When the Sweet Voice of the Father flows over you, you are immediately relieved of all worry.

Sister Hope's health deteriorated quite fast and she dreamt that she was going home. I felt so comforted, I felt no sorrow. While we were alone, I asked her: "Mother, is it normal? I am not crying about mother's departure at all... I have such peace within me". She replied: "My dear Sister in the Lord, it is as it should be, it is the great Comforter... the Holy Spirit. It won't even feel.as though I am away, no... it will just be as if I am in a different place. I got this message from the Father: if sister will stay in this childish naivety, Sister will be surprised by what great things the Lord will do through you."Mother," I asked, "how did the dream end, how did you get out of the car?" She said: "I disappeared from the car and I said to you, now you can walk further, we are on top of the mountain". A few days after that, she crossed over to her Forever Home and I believe the angels carried her in.

18. SUMMARY

I have an unbelievable life within Jesus Christ. As I could give up my husband without placing any pressure on him, the Lord Jesus had picked me up in His arms. Doors opened for me and I am traveling all over to deliver my testimony in aid of others who need strength in their journey to victory in the Lord. I only have two fishes and five loaves, but in His hands, it feeds the crowds.

Prov.14:25: "A truthful witness saves lives."

Many times, when I give testimony to groups, I plead to the Holy Spirit "You take this witness or lead me to the witness which will save a life". And, to mention one example... I have the pleasure to encourage young girls who have kept themselves pure, before marriage. One evening I told them, I was standing in front of the stove, cooking sausage, and as I looked at it, I noticed after I had put water into the pan, that the water and the oil could not mix... the oil was floating on top but the two substances did not amalgamate. I told them how I had mentioned this to Sister Hope and also the thought that entered my mind, which was that it was like my marriage in which I was serving the Lord, but my husband didn't, so we were like water and oil. We didn't fully come together; there wasn't a deeper unity. Sister Hope said;" That is the truth and that must have been the Voice of the Holy Spirit. Even true believers who marry outside the Will of the Father may never achieve that deeper unity as Christ intended for us. Just as oil and water, just float on top of one another, it never mixes to become one person as Christ had instituted marriage. After my husband became converted, I lived in that unity... Not in the flesh, but in Spirit. We would get the same scripture even though we were not together, and we would have the same thoughts etc...You reach a Godly unity."

The one girl was hanging onto my every word... it was as if every word penetrated her mind. A few months afterwards, she sent me an SMS. "Sister, I got your number and I just wanted to say to you that your testimony has saved me from making a very big life mistake. I was engaged and the wedding date had already been set and the wedding venue had also already been reserved. But that evening I realised that although he was a believer, I was missing that unity. I called off the wedding immediately. Thank you very much."

Isiah 54 verse 5 "'For your Maker is your husband – the LORD Almighty is his name – the Holy One of Israel is your Redeemer; He is called the God of all the earth. The LORD will call you back as if you were a wife deserted and distressed in spirit – a wife who married young, only to be rejected, 'says your God."

Isaiah 40 verse 11: "He tends his flock like shepherd: He gathers the lambs in his arms and carries them close to His heart; He gently leads those that have young."

The Lord had taken the imperfect me and made me willing to change. As I heard last week from the Pastor in Knysna, he is also the manager of a large wood factory, and he told us how he takes a large piece of wood to the saw, to have it cut into different pieces to make a chair. Yes, in that same way, I had to let the Master cut off pieces off the old me that had been living just for myself. Today, through His Grace, I can let other tired souls sit in my chair and experience the comfort of Jesus.

The road has also brought me great blessing, because I allowed the Lord to make me into more than just a little stump from the tree, but a chair gives so MUCH MÔRE COMFORT.

Reader, it has been a long and a hard road for me, the road of disobedience; but His Love fetched me from it. Had I kept listening and being obedient, I wouldn't have experienced any of these bad things. I went, did my own thing, like I had wanted it, yet I never had a husband in the true sense of the word. The Father knew everything. I can still hear my father's voice: "Darling, you cannot go and get married, you love to travel too much."

It was the words of Christ! Through His Grace I have become a traveller for Jesus. I have just returned from leave. I was so privileged to have travelled from Velddrif in the West Coast to do His work. I had only been home for one day to do some washing, then I hit the road again to Montague, Ladysmith, George, Knysna and Plettenberg Bay to work for Him, who gave me another chance. Only He can see how happy and grateful I am to be walking with Him again. 'What a Mighty God of restoration do we serve!'

THE LESS PERFECT ME AND THE PERFECT FATHER!

Yes, with teaching from Sister Hope and Jesus Christ who work with me, I am walking on.. right on top of the mountain…

For God so Love the world.

www.ingramcontent.com/pod-product-compliance
Lightning Source LLC
Chambersburg PA
CBHW070207100426
42743CB00013B/3084